THE ORIGINS OF
ITALIAN FASHION
1900–45

THE ORIGINS OF
ITALIAN FASHION

1900–45

Sofia Gnoli

V&A Publishing

First published by V&A Publishing, 2014
Victoria and Albert Museum
South Kensington
London SW7 2RL
www.vandapublishing.com

Distributed in North America by Harry N. Abrams Inc., New York
© The Board of Trustees of the Victoria and Albert Museum, 2014

This translation abridged from *Moda: Dalla nascita della haute couture a oggi*,
by Sofia Gnoli, Copyright © 2012 Carocci editore S.p.A., Roma

The moral right of the author has been asserted.

ISBN 9781 85177 791 4

10 9 8 7 6 5 4 3 2 1
2018 2017 2016 2015 2014

Front jacket/cover illustration: pl.24
Back jacket/cover illustration: pl.41
Frontispiece: Mariano Fortuny; 'Delphos' dress (detail),
pleated silk, silk cord with beads; Italy, *c*.1920; V&A: T.740–1972

Design: VAE Design
Translation: Elizabeth Currie
Copy-editing: Alex Stetter
Index: Hilary Bird

New photography by Richard Davis, V&A Photographic Studio

Printed in China

V&A Publishing

Supporting the world's leading
museum of art and design,
the Victoria and Albert
Museum, London

Contents

Introduction

Italian fashion came of age in the 1950s, but its roots can be traced back much further. There had already been some timid and sporadic attempts to create a national style of fashion, one that was independent of French influences, in the second half of the nineteenth century. In 1848, the journalist Luigi Cicconi proposed a patriotic Italian style of dress and in 1906 the Lombard dressmaker Rosa Genoni, a keen promoter of Italian fashion, presented a collection of clothes inspired by works of art from the Italian Renaissance at the Milan International Exhibition. These initiatives were not followed up, but the issue was addressed again in the early 1920s by Lydia de Liguoro. A famous journalist and editor of the glossy magazine *Lidel*, de Liguoro made many different attempts to launch Italian fashion. Her efforts were unsuccessful, however, and remained linked mainly to ideological and nationalistic issues. In the early 1930s, Paris was still the undisputed centre of fashion. The major Italian dressmakers went to the French capital twice a year, when the new collections were presented, and purchased designs by Chanel and Patou, Lanvin and Madame Vionnet. In 1931, at the height of the depression that followed the Wall Street Crash of 1929, the Fascist regime compiled official statistics that revealed some alarming facts about the clothing imports of 'vain Italian women'. At that point, even Mussolini entered the ring to fight for Italian fashion, declaring in 1932: 'Italian fashion ... still does not exist. We can create it, we must create it.'[1] Inspired by the example set by the *Chambre Syndicale de la Couture Française*,[2] the governing body of the French fashion industry, the regime approved a law to form the *Ente autonomo per la mostra permanente nazionale della moda* (Autonomous Body for the Permanent National Fashion Exhibition) on 22 December 1932. The aim of this new organization was to nationalize the complete fashion production cycle.

Soon after, in 1935, against the background of the Italo-Ethiopian war, the regime changed the organization's name to *Ente nazionale della moda* (National Fashion Body) and gave it more authority. Even though the Body enjoyed immense power in theory, at a practical level its actions were often inconsistent and confused. One of its first initiatives was to introduce the 'mark of guarantee', intended to verify the Italian origins of every garment. On the basis of this complex system, all the dressmakers enrolled in the National Fashion Body were obliged to ensure that a percentage of their designs were of 'national production or creation', or else risk paying heavy fines. The enthusiasm for the campaign for national fashion is symbolized by the *Commentario Dizionario Italiano della Moda*, a fashion dictionary edited by Cesare Meano and published in 1936, which aimed to purge the language of Italian fashion of all foreign terms.

The Origins of Italian Fashion

During World War II, the governments of Allied countries like Great Britain and the United States acknowledged the difficult situation by intervening in the fashion industries. However, because of the Fascist regime's focus on fashion and its potential propaganda value, Italy tried to minimize the problems to such an extent that it is hard to find any references to the war in the Italian fashion press of 1942. On the rare occasions where they can be found, fashion was presented as 'an instrument of motivation for the entire front, a symbol of the certainty that all was going well, of the need to work for a time after victory'.[3] For example, *Bellezza*, 'a monthly magazine of haute couture and Italian life', the official organ of the National Fashion Body, appeared on news-stands for the first time in 1941, six months after Italy entered the war.

If the inconsistencies of Italy's National Fashion Body in some ways stifled initiatives, we should nevertheless recognize the organization's merits. It succeeded in regulating the entire system of fashion production, thereby laying the basis for the future success of a national Italian style.

1

Between French
Haute Couture
and Italian Fashion

From Rose Bertin to Rosa Genoni

Between the second half of the nineteenth century and the beginning of the twentieth, it was impossible to speak of an Italian fashion independent of the French. Apart from a brief period during the Renaissance when Italy was 'master of the world not only in the arts but also in civil life and Beatrice d'Este Duchess of Milan was praised ... as a *novarum vestium inventrix* [inventor of new clothes]',[1] Italy did not dictate fashion. Since the reign of Louis XIV, women's fashion in Europe had been 'Frenchified', so to speak, and until the mid-twentieth century new trends originated mainly in Paris. Even when trends came from other countries, such as the United States or Britain,[2] France was still considered the primary centre for the dissemination of all new styles. From the second half of the seventeenth century onwards, fashion dolls – those inanimate emissaries of French fashion known as *poupées de mode* – were sent out from Paris every year, dressed in the latest styles from the French court.[3]

Until the French Revolution, dressmakers were not considered to be creative innovators, and fashions in clothing were dictated by the courts, whose powerful members were responsible for popularizing them. Only occasionally, and almost by chance, do we know the names of some of the artisans involved. There is documentary evidence for one Agostino, who made clothes for Eleonora di Toledo and the ladies of her court, to be considered among the first Italian dressmakers.[4] In the second half of the eighteenth century, a tailor in Lucca named Matteo Lenzi described himself as 'a ladies' tailor' and Elena Bestini sewed clothes 'in the French fashion'.[5]

More than any other city, Paris was instrumental in promoting the idea of the dressmaker as a designer of clothing. The famous Leroy became popular as the personal dressmaker of the Empress Josephine Bonaparte. A few decades earlier, Rose Bertin,[6] the official modiste of Marie Antoinette, was granted the title 'Minister of Fashion' (pl.2). In 1770 Bertin opened a *magasin de mode* known as Le Grand Mogol in Paris, and within a few years she had become Marie Antoinette's official milliner, to the extent that she put a large sign outside

9

Rose Bertin

her atelier reading '*Marchande de modes de la Reine*'.[7] Her business was highly successful and she soon had hundreds of employees. Thanks to Marie Antoinette, Bertin became a central figure in eighteenth-century fashion. Luxury took on a new meaning as 'elegance was superseded by magnificence, luxury substituted pomp'.[8] This was the moment that fashion began to experiment with the caprices of taste and imagination. Particularly after giving birth to the heir to the throne in 1781, Marie Antoinette began to wear light, fresh fabrics, contrasting with the highly decorated textiles typical of Rococo taste. Despite the simplicity of their fabrics and decorations, the garments were certainly not any cheaper.[9] When the Marquis of Toulongeon took Marie Antoinette to task for the excessive cost of her clothes made of simple fabrics, she pointedly replied: 'Do you pay the artist Vernet only for the canvas and his paints?'[10]

It was another century before dressmakers were accepted as designers in the full sense of the word. Until then, dressmakers continued to work on the basis of a rigorous 'court programme', in accordance with the rules imposed by etiquette. The development of the figure of the *couturier* in the modern sense as a designer of clothing and, as a consequence, the birth of haute couture, took place around the middle of the nineteenth century with the Paris-based Englishman Charles

The Origins of Italian Fashion

3
Donna Franca Florio wearing
a court dress, *c.*1902
Photograph by Foto Fleuren,
Palermo
Galleria del Costume,
Palazzo Pitti, Florence

Frederick Worth (1825–95) (pls 1, 4, 5). In the words of Anne Hollander,
'He worked in a new medium – the complete image of the dressed woman,
not just her dress.'[11] Writing in the newspaper *La Tribuna*, Gabriele D'Annunzio,
supreme chronicler of Italian society, described the great ball held at the Circolo
Nazionale in Rome on 2 February 1885: 'At about 11 o'clock a flash of deity
suddenly illuminated and warmed the air. The Duchess of Sermoneta arrived,
the serene duchess, in a Worthian dress of sky-blue satin, with a veil of the same
colour, starred with silver. A triple-stranded necklace of pearls, diamonds and
emeralds encircled her neck, a diadem encircled her head; other large pearl
drops were arranged in her hair.'[12]

   Worth counted the crowned heads of half of Europe among his clients,
including Queen Victoria and Elisabeth of Austria, as well as the most

4
Worth
Evening dress, pale pink
satin, fastened with laces
at the front and trimmed
with machine-made lace
France, c.1881
V&A: T.34-1973

5
Worth
Evening ensemble, silk velvet,
trimmed with diamanté, lace
France, 1899-1900
V&A: T.459 to B-1974

elegant women in Italy, such as Donna Franca Florio (pls 1, 3), the Countess of Castiglione and Queen Margherita herself.[13] On the occasion of a grand ceremony held at the Palazzo del Quirinale in Rome in 1887, Margherita wore a gorgeous Worth dress, 'lemon-green coloured, decorated with pearls and rhinestones, with a large border of rose leaves around the bottom of the skirts. The shoulders were held in place with diamond and emerald clasps. The train was not long and the gloves were very high.'[14]

Worth was the first to show designs before the start of the season, to sew labels bearing his name inside his clothes, to use models to present his creations and to regularly propose new styles, continually changing fabrics, decorations and designs. With Worth, fashion entered the modern era, becoming at the same time a creative enterprise and an advertising spectacle. If previously clients had directed the dressmaker according to their particular tastes, Worth turned this concept on its head. 'The women who come to me want to ask for my ideas rather than following their own,' he declared. 'If I tell them what is appropriate they do not need any further evidence. My signature on their clothing is sufficient.'[15] Thanks to Worth, during the last decades of the nineteenth century, the romantic silhouette characterized by the crinoline was abandoned for a more streamlined look in which the female body was shaped by a 'serpentine sinuosity', accentuated artificially at the back and highlighted by a tiny wasp-like waist (pl.6).

Even though an authentic style of Italian fashion freed from French dictates dates from the twentieth century, the first isolated attempts to establish independent roots can be traced back to the Italian Unification and the 'vibrant' atmosphere that preceded the revolutionary movements.[16] In 1847, *Moda nazionale*, a quarterly magazine published by Balinghieri in Livorno, declared: 'War, war on the Seine, which has dictated the laws of good taste for so many

7
Rosa Genoni
'Primavera' dress, pale pink satin
with embroidered tulle petticoat
Italy, 1906
Galleria del Costume,
Palazzo Pitti, Florence

centuries. War, war on this damnable domination that overshadows the plants in the garden of the world: war on the opponents of Italian costume.'[17] Shortly afterwards the initiative continued with a more critical mentality, when in 1848 the journalist Luigi Cicconi proposed a patriotic 'Italian-style dress' in Turin's *Il Mondo Illustrato* newspaper, declaring himself a supporter of independence from foreign fashions that with their very names contaminated 'Italian lips'.[18] This initiative was prompted by economic factors as much as political ones: the suggested dress was to be made of velvet, 'the only fabric produced exclusively in the factories of Genoa and Vaprio, following an ancient and authentic artisanal tradition'.[19] After these first attempts did not lead anywhere, the question of an Italian fashion was reformulated many times.

On 26 April 1872, not long after the Italian capital was moved from Florence to Rome, the Italian Society for the Emancipation of Fashion was formed,[20] and the magazine *L'Emporio pittoresco* proclaimed a 'Rebellion against French fashion',[21] but it remained a limited phenomenon. The debate

8
Outfit for a garden party
La Donna, 5 August 1905
Biblioteca Nazionale
Centrale, Rome

9
The Countess of Warwick
La Donna, 5 December 1906
Biblioteca Nazionale
Centrale, Rome

surrounding the need to create a distinctive Italian fashion resurfaced in the early twentieth century, during the world's fairs held in 1906 and 1911 in Milan and Turin respectively. At the International Exhibition in Milan, the Lombard dressmaker Rosa Genoni (1867–1954)[22] promoted a style of Italian fashion freed from French influences by presenting a collection of clothes inspired by paintings by famous Italian Renaissance artists. Before she became a kind of heroine of the nascent Italian fashion scene, Genoni, who was born in Sondrio, had worked for a long time as a *première*[23] in one of Milan's most famous fashion houses, H. Haardt et Fils, which exclusively reproduced French patterns, faithfully copied from sketches 'stolen' or bought at a high price from the most famous Paris ateliers, such as Paquin, Chéruit, Worth, Doucet and Callot Sœurs. Genoni, however, used only Italian textiles in her work. 'Our artistic patrimony should serve as a model for new forms of dress and hairstyles, which would therefore assume a certain taste of classical recollections and a vague nobility of style,' she explained. 'Why is it that our country, which has experienced a regime of freedom for the last thirty years and has witnessed a renewal of industrial and artistic life, still does not have an Italian fashion?'[24] Her creations included a dress inspired by Botticelli's *Primavera*, a gown in pale rose-pink satin silk with an overdress in ivory-coloured tulle embellished with floral-motif embroideries in little pearls, purl, sequins and small golden braids (pl.7). The International Jury awarded it first prize in the decorative arts category.

Like earlier efforts, Genoni's attempts at creating an Italian fashion did not have a widespread effect. One exception was a committee founded in Lombardy in 1909. Called *Una moda di pura arte italiana* (Fashion by pure Italian craft), it included influential businessmen from the textile and clothing industries. The initiatives linked to the 1911 Turin International Exhibition, held on the fiftieth anniversary of Italian Unification, shared the committee's aims. The fashion section of the

exhibition featured arrangements designed by Giorgio Ceragioli, Giovanni Giani and Oreste Pizzo, magnificent spaces with wax mannequins dressed in clothes 'by the most prominent dressmakers, mainly from Turin'.[25] A clear desire to build on the foundations of an Italian fashion emerged from the Turin Fashion Pavilion. A special issue of *La Donna* magazine,[26] published to coincide with the exhibition, declared: 'From now on it will no longer be necessary to travel from our usual place of work or business or embark on long and boring correspondences with the foreign fashion houses in order to dress with utmost elegance.'

However, the most famous Italian fashion houses – Bellenghi, Chiostri Salimbeni, Calò and Emma Paoletti of Florence; Pontecorvo and Maria Berardelli of Rome; Sittich of Trieste; De Gasperi, Rosa & Patriarca and the Bellom Sisters of Turin – continued to slavishly follow the dictates of French fashion, either buying reproduction rights for patterns directly from the French haute couture houses or copying designs from fashion magazines. Italy's major publishers of women's periodicals used French agencies that supplied them with all 'the new and interesting things created in the world of fashion'.[27] Publishers such as Garbini,[28] Sonzogno[29] and Treves[30] distributed different versions of the same title, with varying price points depending on the readership.[31] Examples of this practice include the glossy magazine *Monitore della moda*,[32] published in five different editions, and *Margherita: Giornale delle Signore Italiane*. Published by the Treves brothers, the latter was launched not long after Queen Margherita's coronation in 1878 and named in her honour. Printed on extremely fine paper and enriched with refined engravings, *Margherita* had a luxurious feel and

12
Day suit
La Donna, 25 May 1905
Biblioteca Nazionale
Centrale, Rome

was aimed at a sophisticated, elite readership. The magazine's contributors included Vittorio Bersezio and Matilde Serao, and an annual subscription cost a substantial 24 lire.[33] The cover price was halved for the second edition, 'without fashion-plates and colour supplements'.[34] In order to reach a wider readership Treves launched a cheaper periodical in 1888, *L'eco della moda*,[35] which cost 5 lire a year. It included the same fashion plates as *Margherita*, with the key difference being that they were published about three months later. The message in these periodicals remained French, despite the occasional appearance of Italian fashion plates alongside the usual engravings from France and the first fashion photographs, published towards the end of the first decade of the twentieth century. For example, an article in the March 1909 issue of *La Donna* stated: 'What woman wants, God also wants, and the Parisian lady who epitomizes woman has triumphed again.'

A month later, in a special issue dedicated to fashion, the same magazine listed the high priests of style, including some of the most important French *couturiers*: Worth, Doucet, the Callot Sisters, Dœillet and Drecoll.[36] It is therefore not surprising that in Italy even the language of fashion was rife with Gallic expressions, many of which did not then have an Italian equivalent –

13
Winter sports
La Donna, 20 January 1905
Biblioteca Nazionale
Centrale, Rome

14
Women playing table tennis
La Donna, 5 January 1906
Biblioteca Nazionale
Centrale, Rome

and still do not to this day. Examples of such terms include *ruches, volants, plissés, décolletés, poufs* and *tailleurs*.[37] For this reason, Nino G. Caini, editor of *La Donna*, declared that any attempt to create a distinctive Italian fashion was utopian. However, there were still some who spoke up in its favour, including Olga Ossani, a social chronicler as well as one of the many lovers of Gabriele D'Annunzio. On 3 August 1883, the periodical *Capitan Fracassa* published a striking article by Ossani, entitled *Napoletane* (Neapolitan Women):

> The Parisian lady, who is so much of a woman, with her rich dowry of knowing glances, naive smiles ... revealing and coquettish clothes, lace, ribbons, jewellery, perfumes, seductions, temptations, provocations and malicious actions, can laugh haughtily at the Neapolitan woman, unaware, simple, modest; but if she lent her all her refined weapons, she would find herself with a powerful rival.[38]

Towards a Simpler Style

Until the second decade of the twentieth century, the silhouette of women's clothing harked back to earlier styles, with rare exceptions. The most important fashion innovations of this period reflected the influence of what was known in Italy as the 'Liberty' style,[39] which corresponded with the German *Jugendstil* and art nouveau in France and Belgium. Liberty style became popular in early twentieth-century Italy on a wave of industrialization and the growth of the middle classes, moving away from the typically nineteenth-century tendency to reference historic styles that looked to the past and instead drawing inspiration directly from nature. This led to the linear stylization and the metamorphic and naturalistic features characteristic of fashions of the time. 'The chrysalis', wrote art critic Mario Praz, 'matures for a whole century, and then opens up at the end to reveal the gaudy butterfly: the floral style, Liberty, with the ephemeral life of a butterfly.'[40]

15
Georges Lepape and Paul Poiret
Plate from *Les choses de Paul Poiret vues par Georges Lepape*
France, 1911
V&A: Circ.262-1976

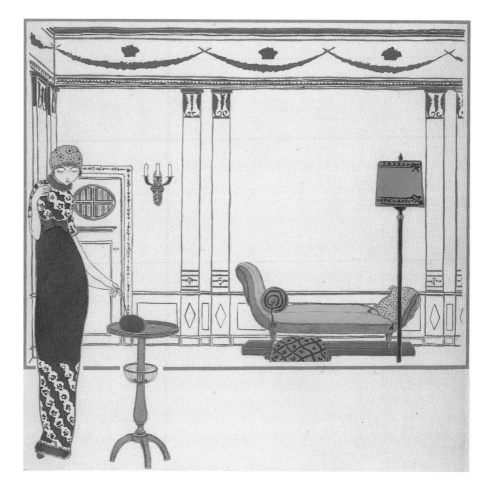

In terms of clothing innovations, Liberty style produced a silhouette vaguely resembling a flower with an undulating stem, gently curving so that women assumed an S-shape, held in tight by a corset that pushed the stomach down and the chest and rear out, with the addition of a bustle. Guido Gozzano referred to this silhouette in his short story *La passeggiata* (The Walk), in which he compares a woman to a flower, echoing the Liberty fashion: 'Moving forwards, holding her body tall like the stem of an old-fashioned flower, she drew her skirt up with one hand – out of habit – revealing with inimitable grace her silk petticoat, of very elegant, varied colours.'[41] Although the early twentieth century did not give rise to a radical shift in fashion, the impulse to free the female body from nineteenth-century constraints became increasingly noticeable.

Encouraged by the growing movement for female emancipation, the first attempts to create less restrictive types of clothing had been made in the second half of the nineteenth century. At a congress held in Stuttgart in 1868, the Council of German Women promoted a more functional kind of dress, while in London in 1881, Viscountess Haberton founded the Rational Dress Society, an organization that proposed reforms in women's dress in the name of health and hygiene and included Oscar Wilde among its members.[42] Amelia Bloomer, one of the pioneers of the American movement for the emancipation of women, was a prominent figure in the United States. In the 1850s she published an article in *The Lily*, the journal she had founded, arguing for the adoption of a more comfortable female garment, a forerunner to trousers: Turkish-style trousers

16
Georges Lepape and Paul Poiret
Plate from *Les choses de Paul
Poiret vues par Georges Lepape*
France, 1911
V&A: Circ.267-1976

worn under a knee-length skirt. This provocative proposal caused a scandal in America, but with the exception of some very restricted circles, Bloomer's ideas did not make much of an impression in Europe.[43]

Apart from the influence of Paul Poiret and the experiments of the Spanish-born Mariano Fortuny in Venice, these movements towards women's dress reform had little impact in Italy. Paralleling developments in the decorative arts, around 1908 there was a counter-trend in dress fashions towards a 'tubular' style, replacing the curvilinear gothic characteristics of art nouveau with a pseudo-classical verticality. Thanks to the dominant vertical line, bodices, corsets and bustles were abandoned, to be replaced by modern underwear. Paul Poiret (1879–1944), the Parisian *couturier* who dominated the international fashion scene for the first two decades of the twentieth century, was one of the most important champions of this revolution in women's dress. The unmatched exponent of a highly original, elegant style made up of classicizing lines and exotic details, Poiret also developed a new form of fashion illustration as well as the concept of the shop window (pls 15, 16). He promoted the creation of a French haute couture syndicate to protect original designs from imitations and distinguished himself as a pioneer of ready-to-wear, creating collections for the department store Printemps. Using his particular vision of good taste to anticipate strategies employed by fashion houses today, Poiret launched the idea of a total lifestyle: not only did he design clothing, he also offered suggestions on the kinds of perfume women should wear or how they should decorate their houses. He was also the first *couturier* to endorse the triumphal entry of art into fashion. 'I am an artist, not a dressmaker,' he said. 'Am I mad when I dream of putting art into my clothes, or when I say that couture is an art?'[44] A great patron and collector, Poiret owned works by Matisse, Picasso, Picabia, Van Dongen and Derain. His designs were inspired by the striking colour contrasts loved by the Fauve painters. He collaborated with painters, photographers and illustrators, from Raoul Dufy to Erté, from Man Ray to Edward Steichen, Paul Iribe and Georges Lepape, all the while referring to the Ballets Russes as a constant aesthetic inspiration. However, after World War I, Poiret's star began to fade. His collections became increasingly luxurious and elaborate, in sharp contrast with the new feminine ideal that had emerged after the war. The world had changed; women had fallen in love with independence, liberty and rationality – concepts that would find their key interpreter in Gabrielle Chanel. So in 1926, having sold his magnificent art collection and on the verge of bankruptcy, Poiret was forced to liquidate his company. He died in 1944, at the age of 65, almost entirely forgotten. Despite this, his eccentric and extravagant designs were periodically reinterpreted in the world of fashion, for example in the work of Elsa Schiaparelli or Walter Albini, that pioneer of 'Made in Italy', by Gianni Versace and John Galliano – all designers who, at different times, were profoundly influenced by Poiret.

Mariano Fortuny and Maria Monaci Gallenga

A painter, set designer, costume maker, inventor, photographer and collector, Mariano Fortuny y Madrazo was above all an artist-*couturier*, eclectic and genial by nature. He was born in Granada in 1871, a child of art: his father was Mariano Fortuny y Marsal, a famous Spanish painter who died when Fortuny was three. After spending his early childhood between Rome and Paris, the young Fortuny became an adopted Venetian when his mother, Cecilia de Madrazo y Garreta, moved to the city in 1889. He had inherited his father's artistic talent, and at the beginning of the twentieth century he opened a small silk-printing workshop. His first creations included veils, shawls and so-called 'Knossos' scarves, printed with decorative motifs influenced by Cretan art. Fortuny went on to create textiles printed with oriental, classical and Renaissance-inspired designs. In 1909 he patented a type of polychrome print, combining gold and silver dust made with copper and aluminium with natural dyes such as madder and dyer's weed.

Classical art was Fortuny's main source of inspiration: the name of his most famous design, the 'Delphos' dress, is a reference to the Charioteer of Delphi, the life-size bronze statue discovered at the Temple of Apollo in Delphi in 1896. The dress was made of a long cylinder of very light satin or pleated silk taffeta, which enfolded and highlighted the female form. The unique nature of the 'Delphos' gown lay in the particular type of pleats used to make it. Patented by the artist-*couturier* in 1909, the Fortuny pleat formed the basis of another famous garment: the 'Peplos', which was inspired by a kind of tunic with an irregular, diagonal hem worn by korai figures. To help it hang better, the gown

was embellished with small Murano glass beads. The innovative nature of the Fortuny pleat inspired the work of many later designers, such as the twisted garments designed by Nanni Strada (b.1941) or the reinterpretation of the 'Delphos' dress that Issey Miyake (b.1938) produced for his *Pleats Please* line.

Usually made in muted tones such as sea green or pale rose, Fortuny's clothes created unusual iridescences and highlighted every part of the body. The garments were therefore often considered to be immodest, and the women brave enough to wear them were eccentric and extravagant, such as Isadora Duncan, Peggy Guggenheim and Eleonora Duse. The Marchesa Luisa Casati Stampa caused a sensation by wearing a 'Delphos' gown (pl.17) to the famous Longhi ball in 1913.

Unlike Poiret's creations, Fortuny's garments were unconnected to the fashions of the time and fascinated aesthetes and artists, such as Marcel Proust and Gabriele D'Annunzio. In 1910, D'Annunzio described an outfit worn by Isabella, the heroine of his novel *Forse che sì forse che no* (Maybe Yes, Maybe No): 'She was wearing one of those delicate tunics with minute pleats printed by an ingenious creator with marine motifs from Mycenaean art.' Proust repeatedly returned to Fortuny in his *In Search of Lost Time*. 'As for her toilette,' he wrote of Albertine, 'at that time she liked Fortuny's clothes most of all.'[45] Proust saw these garments as particularly evocative:

> These Fortuny gowns, faithfully antique but markedly original, brought before the eye like a stage setting, with an even greater suggestiveness than a setting, since the setting was left to the imagination, that Venice loaded with the gorgeous East from which they had been taken, of which they were, even more than a relic in the shrine of Saint Mark suggesting the sun and a group of turbaned heads, the fragmentary, mysterious and complementary colour. Everything of those days had perished, but everything was born again, evoked to fill the space between them with the splendour of the scene and the hum of life, by the reappearance, detailed and surviving, of the fabrics worn by the Doges' ladies.[46]

After Fortuny's death in 1949, his wife Adele Henriette Nigrin donated their home on San Beneto square, Ca' Pesaro degli Orfei, to the city of Venice, and it is now the site of the Fortuny Museum.[47]

Following in Fortuny's footsteps – interweaving art and fashion, handmade technique and creativity – Rosa Giolli Menni (1889–1975) in Milan and Maria Monaci Gallenga (1880–1944) in Rome continued to develop a purely Italian style. Menni developed batik techniques to make clothing and soft furnishings, while Gallenga built on the research of the 'wizard' of pleats. However, Gallenga was perhaps more attentive to developments in taste than Fortuny, and showed greater commitment to asserting an Italian fashion independent of the French than he had (pl.18).

Born into an intellectual bourgeois family, Gallenga focused on printed textiles. Working mainly on velvets, georgettes and silk crêpes in jewel tones such as sapphire blue, amethyst violet and ruby red, she used an exclusive technique involving metal pigments, which she patented. Her patterned textiles were created by hand, using special stencils to print directly onto the finished garment in order to adapt the design to its form and cut.[48] In 1913, she was one of the artists who took part in the *Secessione Romana* exhibitions, alongside Gino Sensani, Galileo Chini, Marcello Piacentini and Romano Romanelli, among others. Together they supported the programme initiated by the *Ente nazionale per l'artigianato e la piccola industria* (National Body for Craft and Small Industries) to promote the image of Italian products. Shortly afterwards, Gallenga opened the *Bottega d'arte italiana* (Italian Art Workshop) at 6 via Veneto, Rome. Somewhere between a shop and an art gallery, this was a highly modern space in which Gallenga sold her own designs and exhibited work by other artists.

Gallenga's activities to help promote a distinctive Italian style continued into the 1920s. Having successfully taken part in the 1925 Paris Exhibition, in 1928 she opened the *Boutique Italienne* in Paris with Bice Pittoni and Carla Visconti di Modrone. The shop on rue Miromesnil served as a showcase for the best Italian art and craft products. It closed in 1934.[49] In the 1970s, the Gallenga archive was taken over by Umberto Tirelli, the great tailor and costumier for theatre and film. As well as being used in many plays, Gallenga's pieces were also referenced in the field of fashion. Around 1980, the Fendi sisters chose prints by Gallenga to create a series of fabrics for their accessories collection. 'My Fendi friends, diabolically, very cunningly, often hang around in my stores,' Tirelli said. 'One day they discovered Gallenga's capes, the original fabrics, the prints. They understood and suggested printing velvets for evening bags.'[50]

18
Maria Monaci Gallenga
Mantle, printed silk velvet
Italy, c.1922
V&A: T.435-1977

2

The 'Fashion Battles'

War and the Birth of the Modern Woman

> War has been the principal driving force behind women's progress. The weaker sex has learnt how to be strong. And out of the houses where doll-like women reigned have emerged working women (with their hair tied up at the neck and skirts substituted with trousers where necessary), tram drivers, cart drivers, road sweepers, nurses, farmers, railway and office workers.[1]

After World War I, there was a parting of the ways between the older and younger generations (pls 20, 21). In order to save their economies, the countries involved in the conflict were forced to employ women in agriculture, industry and the service sector, overturning the traditional division of labour between the sexes. Between 1914 and 1917, there were three million women working in industry, 700,000 of whom had taken on men's jobs.[2] Working in sectors that had until then been exclusively reserved for men led to the need for more practical clothing, appropriate for the new role that women were gaining in society.[3] Various types of underwear that restricted freedom of movement, such as the corset, were the first items to be eliminated. 'Now fashion is simple, suits in thick blue or grey wool, an entirely youthful fashion, because the very short skirts, the shoes and little boots, almost like buskins, will not tolerate decadence, they require beautiful ankles and daring,' *Margherita* noted in March 1916. 'Femininity seems rather masculine and uniformed.'[4]

In the 1920s, the new role model of the emancipated woman gained prominence. Anglophone countries saw the rise of the flapper, while in France they were called *garçonnes*. The term flapper used in this context first appeared in print in 1903, in a comic novel by Desmond Coke called *Sandford of Merton: A Story of Oxford Life*, a parody of a classic children's book, *The History of Sandford and Merton,* published in the 1780s by Thomas Day. The flapper in question was a young and unconventional girl who drank, smoked and danced in such a way that the rustling of her dress recalled the flapping noise made by little birds as they learn to fly (pl.19). This stereotype of the 'modern girl' also owed something to the work of F. Scott Fitzgerald and the roles played in silent films by actresses such as Louise Brooks or Clara Bow. As the star of *It* (1927),[5] a traditional comedy based on a story by Elinor Glyn, Bow is soon transformed into the prototype of the flapper. Her character, Betty Lou, became the model for

19
Loris Riccio
Illustration for Radice,
Lidel, Christmas issue, 1924
Biblioteca Nazionale
Centrale, Rome

Max Fleischer's animated character *Betty Boop*, the first sexy heroine of American cartoons, who made her screen debut in 1930.

In France it was Victor Margueritte who coined the term *garçonne* in his novel of the same name, published in 1922. It was read enthusiastically by thousands of women fascinated by the adventures of a Sorbonne student who not only steals a man's jacket and tie but the rest of his clothes too.[6] The story helped to popularize an ideal of slim, androgynous femininity, quite the opposite of the more florid look popular at the start of the century. 'In the past, women were architectural like the prow of a ship,' said Poiret, 'now they resemble small, malnourished telegraph operators.'[7] *Lidel* magazine expanded on this observation in May 1925: 'It would appear that the female form itself has been changed. Among the young, you hardly ever see Juno-esque women any more. In order to be admired and adulated by suitors today it is necessary to have the air of long, thin, flattened sardines' (see pl.19).

In this decade, the most original developments in fashion were rising hemlines, with skirts barely covering the knees appearing between 1925 and 1926, putting legs and stockings into the spotlight; the introduction of sandals; the abolition of sleeves and the *garçonne* haircut (pl.22). 'Women came home carrying their shorn locks in a parcel,' journalist Irene Brin recalled. 'Hair was curled and cut close to the neck, shoes were very comfortable and jacket collars came up high to reveal just a glimpse of round black eyes and lips painted blood-red ... Season by season, women fell in love with their freedom.'[8]

Fashion became more accessible and democratic in the 1920s and its key figures, such as Patou, Chanel and Jeanne Lanvin, were still French. Lanvin created the first line of clothing for children, while Patou[9] and Chanel made their names as exponents of the burgeoning taste for sportswear (see pl.37). While Chanel gave women modern clothing, Madeleine Vionnet[10] introduced international fashion to a unique classicizing style, with a timeless touch. 'If it is possible to speak of a Vionnet school nowadays, it is above all because I have shown myself to be an enemy of fashion,' she said. 'In the fleeting whims of the seasons, there is an element of superficiality and instability that scandalized my sense of beauty.'[11] Shabby and plump, Vionnet did not possess Chanel's charm. 'I have never been worldly ... and it has never been important to me to dress well,' she confessed. Despite this, she gently upturned the aesthetic codes of her time and gave women a new freedom with her bias-cut clothes that highlighted natural curves. Diana Vreeland described her as 'the most important dressmaker of the twentieth century'.[12]

Lydia de Liguoro and Fortunato Albanese: Pioneers of Italian Fashion

Despite continuing efforts to launch Italian fashion, France maintained its leading position in the fashion sector during the 1920s – it was no coincidence that only French patterns were illustrated in Italian women's periodicals. On 16 March 1919 the first national congress on clothing commerce was held at the Palazzo Campidoglio in Rome, under the auspices of the Ministry for Industry and Commerce. The principal aim of the congress was to achieve freedom from the absolute domination of France, as the organizing committee underlined in its report: 'Given that we do not lack either appeal or good taste ... we need to try and establish our country within the orbit of the radiating centres of Fashion and Clothing.'[13] The congress concluded on 18 March, approving the nomination of a commission to present the government with 'a complete outline for the structure of a National Institute of Clothing' and a Fashion Body.[14] However, either because of a lack of unanimous support from clothing manufacturers or the after-effects of the resignation of the Prime Minister Vittorio Emanuele Orlando, the project came to nothing.

Two pioneers in the Italian 'fashion battles'[15] emerged over the course of the congress: Fortunato Albanese and Lydia de Liguoro. In 1917, the former, who had been pushing for fashion independence since 1912, presented the Minister for Industry with a leaflet entitled *Per una moda italiana*.[16] In 1918, Albanese went on to write a report on the rationale behind the first national congress of the clothing industries.[17] The following year, he gave lectures on the social and economic significance of fashion.[18] Lydia de Liguoro launched the magazine

22
John Guida
Illustration for Coen department
stores, 1924
Giordani Aragno Collection

23
Eduardo Garcia Benito
Illustration for *Lidel*,
15 March 1924
Biblioteca Nazionale
Centrale, Rome

Lidel in May 1919. The name was both her pseudonym and an acronym of the different sections of the magazine: the letters stood for *letture, illustrazioni, disegni, eleganza, lavoro* (literature, illustrations, designs, elegance, work). According to its founder, *Lidel* (pls 23–7) represented the 'will of a woman's mighty heart, turning to the best of Italian women to help them appreciate all our beautiful and noble things, encouraging all our artistic creators in favour of our own style of fashion.'[19] De Liguoro was a fervent but rather inconsistent nationalist and in 1919 she joined the Milanese Women Fascists, a group that advocated for a league against luxury to counter the economic crisis caused by the war. Not long after founding her luxurious magazine, she was promoting a propaganda campaign against luxury with the slogan 'Do not buy'.

24
Filiberto Mateldi
Illustration for Lino Manzoni
knitwear, *Lidel*, 15 June 1925
Biblioteca Nazionale
Centrale, Rome

Fazzoletto gigolette

25
Francesco Dal Pozzo
Fazzoletto gigolette, illustration
for Iris Milano, *Lidel*,
15 June 1923
Biblioteca Nazionale
Centrale, Rome

The following year De Liguoro represented the National Women Fascists in Milan at the second congress of the garment industries held in Rome. Faced with attacks from manufacturers and retailers who were alarmed by the possible consequences of an anti-luxury campaign, she wrote in her concluding report to the congress that 'there is no need to combat luxury in general, only luxury imported from abroad'. The initiatives of this 'league against luxury' included the Genoese magazine *La Chiosa* calling a referendum to adopt a single type of clothing – the *tailleur*, or suit; the ball hosted by the Countess Rucellai at her Florentine palace at which guests were obliged to wear the *tuta* or overalls designed by Thayaht; and Filippo Tommaso Marinetti's manifesto *Against Female Luxury*, which was published in 1919.

De Liguoro's activities were much admired by Mussolini, who sent her a telegram in 1920: '*Lidel* – fine and beautiful – is also a force working towards our common objective: the affirmation of Italy and Italian-ness across the world.'[20] In the same year, Italian outfits by Ferrario (pl.27),[21] Radice, Fumach and Ventura[22] were on show in the fashion pavilion of the Milan trade fair, alongside sophisticated designs from the usual French fashion houses. Vittorio Montano, the owner of Ventura and the director of the Union of Haute Couture,[23] gave a lucid analysis of the Italian fashion industry and its subordination to French fashion, concluding:

> As far as possible let us shake off this game, which lowers us to the level of copiers, which absorbs so much of our energies in 'patterns', and which sometimes necessitates a wretched 'pilfering'. If we refined our artistic and overall culture, we would feel stronger to embark on this journey, which has been attempted unsuccessfully up until now.[24]

At the same time, a growing number of Italian department stores were selling goods at fixed prices. One of the first was La Rinascente – the store's name, meaning 'rebirth', was chosen by the writer Gabriele D'Annunzio (see pl.33) – which was founded in 1917 by the Borletti family, who had taken over the stores owned by the Bocconi brothers.[25] In 1919 the department store UPIM (*Unico Prezzo Italiano Milano*) was launched, financed with proceeds from La Rinascente. First established in 1931, the Standard chain of stores changed its name to Standa in 1937 during the Fascist regime's campaign of Italianization.

These large department stores – which were soon joined by the smaller Castelnuovo, Coen, Zingone and Magazzini Italiani – did not become completely established until after the war.[26] However, unlike their American counterparts, which served a rich and privileged clientele, they were, together with the usual seamstresses, the preferred destination of middle-class women.

26
Francesco Dal Pozzo
Illustration for Salterio & Co.,
Lidel, Christmas issue, 1924
Biblioteca Nazionale
Centrale, Rome

27 *opposite*
Loris Riccio
Advertisement for Ferrario,
Lidel, February 1924
Biblioteca Nazionale
Centrale, Rome

C. Ferrario

Milano
Corso Vittorio Emanuele, 31

*Inizia
l' esposizione
della
nuova collezione*
Primavera-Estate
*a partire dal
12 marzo.*

LORIS
RICCIO
924

LE LYS NOIR

ROBE DU SOIR, DE MADELEINE VIONNET

Nº 5 de la Gazette. Année 1923. Planche 24
Modèle déposé. Reproduction interdite.

Cross-Fertilizations: The Influence of Futurism

The Futurists turned fashion into an important field of inquiry in order to
destroy the old balance and overturn suffocating 'bourgeois traditions'.[27] Artists
such as Giacomo Balla (pls 30, 31), Fortunato Depero, Thayaht and Filippo
Tommaso Marinetti, the movement's founder, became interpreters of a new style
that broke with the past, and whose aim was to reflect 'the dynamism, energy and
speed emblematic of modern times'.[28]

The Futurists declared their views on clothing in various articles as well
as specific manifestos. One example was Balla's *Futurist Manifesto on Menswear*,
first published towards the end of 1913 in French before being translated into
Italian with the striking title *Il vestito antineutrale* (Anti-Neutral Clothing),
in line with the interventionist ideals of Futurism. In this manifesto Balla
banned 'all faded, sweet, neutral, strange, dark colours ... striped, diplomatic
prints [and] symmetrical cuts'.[29] In the context of nationalist interventionism,

two articles by Arnaldo Ginna were of particular importance. Entitled *Donne italiane riprofumate il mondo coi profumi italiani* (Italian Women Re-Perfume the World with Italian Scents) and *Calci al nemico con scarpe italiane* (Kicking the Enemy with Italian Shoes), they were published in *L'Italia Futurista* in July and August 1916 respectively. Ginna proposed a new type of clothing that could only be achieved with the rebirth of Italian industry. In 1920, Volt (Vincenzo Fani) drew up the *Manifesto della moda femminile futurista* (Futurist Manifesto of Womenswear), which began: 'Womenswear has always been more or less Futurist. Fashion is the female equivalent of Futurism. Speed, novelty, the courage of creation.' The manifesto covered themes such as genius, daring and economy. In the first section, Volt called for fashion to be recognized as an art form, on the same level as architecture and music. In the second, extravagance was considered fundamental, while the third section began by stating that 'the new fashions will be affordable to all beautiful women whose numbers, in Italy, are legion'. Against the background of the economic crisis provoked by the war, the *Manifesto* proposed that costly fabrics should be abandoned and replaced with cheap materials such as glue, card, tin foil, hemp and fish skin. In the same

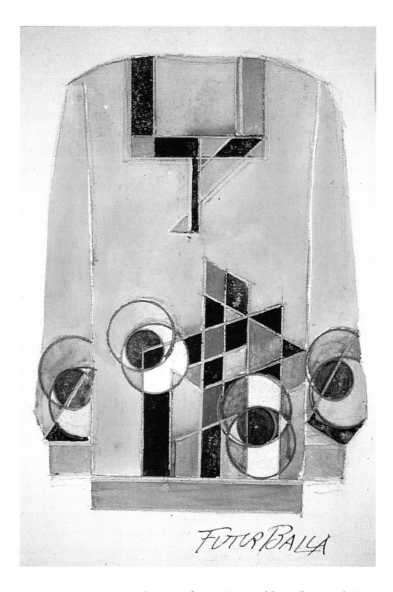

year, Marinetti wrote the manifesto *Contro il lusso femminile* (Against Female Luxury). He railed against 'the morbid mania for luxury' that afflicted many women, consisting of the desire for jewels, fabrics, sweets, silks, velvets, perfumes and furs.

Futurist fashion creations met with much greater success abroad than in Italy. Masquerading as French products, typically Futurist designs were presented at the 1925 Paris Exhibition, at dizzying prices. 'For the first time coloured furs and Futurist cloaks appeared in Paris,' Balla and Jannelli said in an interview published in *L'Impero* in June 1925. 'Futurist buttons could be seen at the Casa Bauer of Paris stand ... little bags and shoes ... at the Casa Brusk of Paris stand.'[30] The success of Futurist 'fashion' abroad was partly due to the growing significance of collaborations between fashion designers and members of artistic and literary movements, particularly in France. Important examples included Elsa Schiaparelli and Coco Chanel, whose names became linked with the Surrealists and the Cubists respectively. Schiaparelli turned to Surrealist artists, particularly Salvador Dalí, often dressing his wife, Gala, in exchange for new ideas and original designs.[31] Chanel collaborated with Jean Cocteau on several occasions,

32
Thayaht
La Vague, illustration of a
bathing suit by Madeleine
Vionnet, *La Gazette du
bon ton*, no. 3, 1923
V&A: NAL

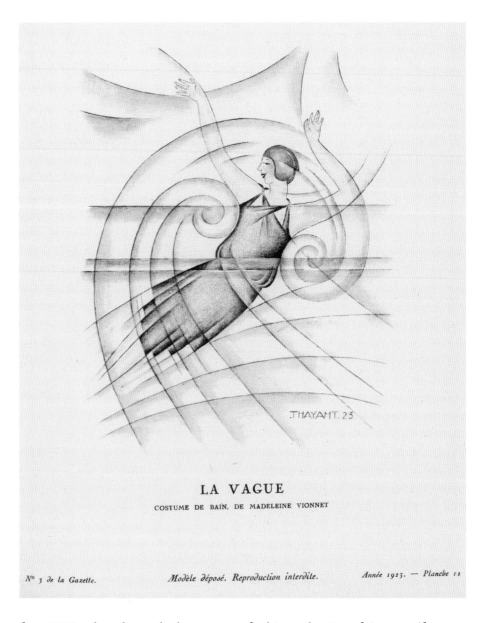

LA VAGUE

COSTUME DE BAIN, DE MADELEINE VIONNET

N° 3 de la Gazette.   *Modèle déposé. Reproduction interdite.*   *Année 1923. — Planche 11*

from 1922, when she made the costumes for his production of *Antigone* (for which Pablo Picasso created the scenery), until 1937, when she designed the costumes for *Oedipus Rex*.

Thayaht (the pseudonym used by artist and designer Ernesto Michahelles, 1893–1959) created the *tuta*, or overalls, in 1919. Due to the small amount of fabric required to make this garment and the minimal wastage involved, the *tuta* fitted in with the mentality of the poor economy in the period immediately after World War I. Despite its innovative nature and the 'economy of time' the *tuta* represented, as it was so quick to put on – 'it clothes your whole body: with only seven buttons and a simple belt you are already done' – this garment was a short-lived invention in the panorama of Futurist fashion interventions.[32] However, in the same year Thayaht began working as the official illustrator for Vionnet, embarking on a dynamic and fruitful fashion collaboration. Over the course of a few years, Thayaht created Vionnet's logo and designs for textiles and clothes that were characterized by a great sense of dynamism, using spirals and centrifugal lines (pls 28, 29, 32). The classical allusions typical of Vionnet were reconfigured for a modern universe, with references to functionality, travel and sport. One example was the *Giocatrice di golf* (Female golfer) Thayaht designed for Vionnet in 1923, which he also published in *La Gazette du bon ton* under the title '*Pour le golf*'. In 1928 the National Fascist Group of Straw Workers asked Thayaht to design straw hats, and the following year he started working with the National Fascist Federation of the Clothing Industry and with *Moda*, the Federation's official magazine.[33] In the spirit of the regime, Thayaht was increasingly in favour of a 'new' and 'national' fashion, as he explained in a number of articles. For example, in a piece entitled *Estetica del vestire: Moda solare, Moda futurista* (Aesthetics of Dress: Solar Fashion, Futurist Fashion), published in 1930, he wrote about the need to 'have the courage to create a new law of fashion, intimately linked with our landscape'.[34]

In 1932, Thayaht and his brother Ram (Ruggero Michahelles) were among the authors of the *Manifesto per la trasformazione dell'abbigliamento maschile* (Manifesto for the Transformation of Menswear). This document demonstrated a strong interest in the clothing industry, while proclaiming the need 'for men to have the same freedom in clothing that women have enjoyed for some time'. Not by chance, the Manifesto concluded with a specific hope for the future: 'We expect intelligent and effective collaboration from the Italian clothing companies, who will understand the importance of our initiative given its rich commercial possibilities, in order to produce and launch on a large scale the new synthetic Futurist clothing.'[35] As part of the process of evaluating the possibilities of Italian fashion, a competition to design a Futurist hat was launched in March 1933, presided over by Marinetti. The edition of *Futurismo* published that same month featured the 'Futurist Manifesto of the Italian Hat',[36] a piece written by Marinetti with Francesco Monarchi, Enrico Prampolini and Mino Somenzi, the editor of *Futurismo*. As well as declaring the superiority of the Italian race, the authors emphasized the global superiority of the 'Italian hat'. They argued for its return, given that many Italians had recently adopted foreign ways, going out with 'naked heads' in the American style. Against the backdrop of the Manifesto's promoting a rebirth of the Italian hat, we must highlight the valuable contribution made by Borsalino, a company that in 1934 introduced the 'aerodynamic hat'.[37] The company's name became synonymous with a particular type of men's felt hat, which was famously worn by Humphrey Bogart in the film *Casablanca* (1942). In 1970 it became even more famous with the release of a film called *Borsalino*, starring Jean-Paul Belmondo and Alain Delon.

The year 1933 also saw the publication of the 'Futurist Manifesto on the Italian Tie', drafted by Renato Di Bosso and Ignazio Scurto. Described as a 'slipknot' or 'real noose', the tie was to be banned from menswear, substituted by a patriotic 'anti-tie made from very light, durable, shining metal'.[38] Other contributors to Futurist fashion were the painter Gerardo Dottori, who designed clothing during the Fascist era, and Fortunato Depero, who wrote a manifesto entitled 'The Clothing of Victory' in 1942.[39]

3

Femme Fatale or Perfect Housewife?

Royal Weddings

The Roaring Twenties came to a tragic end with the Wall Street Crash of 1929. The model of the androgynous *donna crisi* (woman in crisis) died out over the course of this decade, to be replaced by a new 'siren woman'. At the catwalk shows, the female chest and waist, forgotten about in the 1920s, were emphasized again and hemlines dropped below the knee once more (pl.33). In 1930, the Royal Household and Il Duce's family contributed to the prominence of Italian fashion with two weddings. The magnificent wedding of Prince Umberto of Savoy, the heir to the throne, and Maria José of Belgium took place on 8 January. The bride wore a white velvet gown, which was based on a sketch by Prince Umberto and made by the Ventura atelier.[1] The veil was from Bruges, a gift from the people of Belgium. The Italian essence of Maria José's dress was emphasized in an article written and illustrated by John Guida in *Fantasie d'Italia*:

> The blonde Princess, whose family home borders on France, could have brought from Paris a whole blossoming of traditional elegance, renewing the glories of those dressmakers who have enjoyed the triumphs of two Empires. Instead, with exquisite sentiment that shows her attachment to her new nation, she has chosen to have her wedding gown and all her trousseau of marvellous dresses made in Italy with Italian goods and by Italian dressmakers.[2]

On 24 April of the same year, Count Galeazzo Ciano and Mussolini's daughter Edda, who wore a gown by Montorsi,[3] celebrated their more modest wedding (pls 34–6). Over the course of this decade, the regime paid increasing attention to clothing. While the first attempts to create an Italian style had been dictated by essentially nationalistic motives, economic factors became more significant during the 1930s.[4] Thanks to official statistics compiled by the regime in 1931, it was discovered that Italy imported clothing goods worth one billion lire annually, absorbing about one third of French exports.[5] In order to reduce foreign imports, it was essential to increase appreciation of Italian fashion. Consequently, the regime approved a new law on 22 December 1932 to create an Autonomous Body for the Permanent National Fashion Exhibition,[6] with initial

33
Marcello Dudovich
Poster for La Rinascente
department stores, c.1935
Massimo & Sonia Cirulli Archive,
New York

45

funding of about two million lire. The new body's key task was to organize the different clothing sectors so that the complete cycle of fashion production could take place within Italy.

'Towards an Italian fashion' was Mussolini's command, as published in *Popolo d'Italia* in November 1932. According to Lydia de Liguoro, 'His interest and voice was necessary to revive, among those who have been fighting for it for so long, the hope of finally seeing a national fashion embark on the road to a serious independent organization.'[7]

Fashion Pages

Women's magazines, of which there were an increasing number in Italy at this time, played a vital role in the dissemination of fashion. They also provide a great deal of evidence of Fascism's frequently inconsistent attitudes towards women. The regime did not approve of the youthful *garçonne* style, a look it described as *donna crisi*, and tried to replace it with the florid ideal of the 'exemplary wife and mother'.[8] The regime promoted a huge anti-slimming campaign in order to build up throngs of women who, as Irene Brin noted, were subsisting on 'salads and oranges, without oil or sugar … they weighed themselves, they compared waist sizes, they talked about the difficulty of following a diet in the home, dreamt of leaving for famous health spas, where fasting was allowed and monitored'.[9] In an article published in *Critica Fascista* in 1930, Mario Pompei described the nefarious effects of the *garçonne* fashion:

All of us, among our small circle of acquaintances, know fine young
girls who have shortly succumbed to tuberculosis or at the least to
unhealthy organic deteriorations, because of a desire to look like the
spineless giraffes that the latest fashion houses have launched onto the
fashion market as the ultimate models.[10]

The regime's preference for curves was driven by the idea that thin
women did not appeal to men, that Latin beauty was naturally rounded and
that women 'in crisis' could not produce strong and healthy progeny for the
homeland (pl.38). 'The place of honour for a man is on the battlefield,' wrote

Alfredo Oriani, 'women's place of honour is at the pillow of a child; different natures, different duties, different standards.'[11]

Among the magazines aimed at women, *Lidel*[12] (pl.39) was one of the first to publicize the regime's anti-slimming campaign. An issue from 1932 included a number of unusually curvy models:

> These fashion-plates are our contribution ... to the anti-slimming campaign promoted following the Medical Congress and we hope they demonstrate conclusively that there is no incompatibility between recent fashions and a healthy and balanced development of those curves that give women the soft grace they have been so proud of for centuries and have only been forced to deny over the last ten years.[13]

Lidel's motto became 'Slender not thin'; the idea of being thin was to be 'discarded'.[14]

39
Enrico Sacchetti
Cover of *Lidel*, May 1919
Biblioteca Nazionale
Centrale, Rome

Femme Fatale or Perfect Housewife?

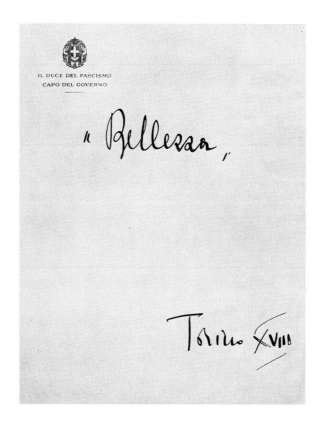

As well as a high-end magazine like *Lidel*, titles such as *La Donna*, which was launched in 1905, also proposed a similar approach for their more modest readership. Other publications along the same lines included *Cordelia*, which merged with *La Donna* in 1942;[15] *Rakam*; *Lei*, which became *Annabella* in 1937, during the regime's campaign against the pronoun *lei*; *Sovrana*, which changed its name to *Grazia* in 1938; and *Moda*, the official periodical of the National Fascist Federation of the Clothing Industry, which was replaced in 1941 by *Bellezza*, a luxury glossy magazine. The first issue, published in January 1941, declared: '*Bellezza* will continue to pursue, with the same willpower and unconditional love, the work begun by *Moda* ... to endorse Italian craft and industry, in order to create a fashion that is truly ours' (pl.40).

In addition to these magazines, titles such as *Vita femminile* and *Dea* were even more direct in expressing the voice of the regime. Launched in Rome in 1922, *Vita femminile* was a monthly publication covering fashion and culture. It was perhaps the first magazine that, thanks to its editor Ester Lombardo, took a close-up view of the fashion industry. The markedly Fascist *Dea*, a monthly magazine launched in 1933, set out to 'highlight Italian products and to counteract the invasion of foreign fashion magazines'.[16]

The regime attempted to use publications such as these to impose a 'national' fashion on Italy, increasingly through the use of censorship: by 1934 some periodicals had already started to omit the names of the Parisian fashion houses whose patterns they published, and by 1937 all references to foreign *couturiers* had disappeared and only Italian designs were featured. Yet wealthier women still bought magazines like *Vogue*, *Harper's Bazaar* and *Marie Claire* via Switzerland and spent fortunes on dresses by the best French ateliers, only wearing Italian creations for the regime's official events.

The Hollywood Model and *Telefoni Bianchi*

Cinema was another important vehicle for the dissemination of fashion.
As a result, the regime's interest in the clothing industry also had significant
repercussions for the world of celluloid. Until the 1930s, the costumes for Italian
films were usually conceived by the set designer and made by the wardrobe
mistress, but now the separate role of the costume designer began to emerge.[17]

In 1937, the regime attempted to make actresses' costumes conform to its
sartorial ideals by legally requiring all film production companies to use clothing
with a 'mark of guarantee' from the National Fashion Body,[18] but it was not able

Concorso ippico

to compensate for problems that were already well entrenched in Italian cinema. One of the main issues was its lack of stars. The complete control the regime had over cinema in the 1930s and 1940s meant that no legendary figures had been created other than that of Il Duce himself: 'Mussolini ... sucked the blood out of his own image, so that he became the image, so that his citizen-consumers' attention converged upon his figure, making not only Fascism as a movement the subject of his communication, but also the Duce as a person.'[19]

Instead, Italian women tried to identify with Hollywood heroines, although sometimes in a rather confused way, as the journalist Leo Longanesi noted:

> Women look for style in Dietrich (the floral sphinx) or Harlow (the pagan typist), but in vain. They oscillate between old Europe and America, they throw themselves wherever they see a costume but then they cannot give it a face. 'Should we wear a veil again? Chew gum? Low heels? Jumper or ermine? Directoire or peasant wear? At the wheel of a car or picking daisies in the meadows? The woman of 1937 doesn't know.'[20]

In the 1930s, costume designers such as Adrian, Travis Banton, Howard Greer, Edith Head and Orry Kelly, among many others, dictated the international seasonal trends more than the great French fashion houses. They were responsible for the dreams of thousands of women, who wanted to wear the costumes of their favourite heroine as soon as they had finished watching a film. As Edith Head[21] explained, the costume designer was 'as important as the star. When you said Garbo you thought of Adrian; when you said Dietrich, you said Banton. The magic of an Adrian or Banton dress was part of the selling of a picture. Sets, costumes and makeup just aren't considered the art forms they used to be.'[22]

'New York and Paris justifiably looked down their august noses at the dresses we designed in Hollywood,' Howard Greer recalled. 'Well maybe they were vulgar, but they did have imagination.'[23] Costume designers were in fact not able to take much inspiration from the great French dressmakers: as months passed between the start of filming and the appearance of the finished product on the big screen, they somehow had to predict the fashions of the future.

Adrian Adolph Greenberg (1903–59), known as Adrian, was one of the most successful costume designers in Hollywood. As well as being the head of costume at MGM (Metro Goldwyn Mayer) from 1928 to 1941, he created the looks of some of the biggest stars of the 1930s, including Greta Garbo and Joan Crawford. In order to hide Crawford's physical imperfections, characterized by an imposing bust and short legs, Adrian decided to emphasize the breadth of her 'Johnny Weissmuller style'[24] shoulders even more by dressing her in jackets with bulky shoulder pads. The actress's metamorphosis took place on the set of *Letty Lynton* (1932) and was an immediate success (pl.43). In the season following the film's release, the department store Macy's sold more than 50,000 copies of the upside-down triangle-shaped dress the actress wore in the film. More significantly, the great fashion designer Elsa Schiaparelli had shown a similar style in Paris the previous year without causing a sensation. This single example helps indicate the scale of cinema's influence on fashion. Faced with such unexpected popularity, Adrian declared in an interview: 'Whoever would have thought

my career depended on Crawford's shoulders?'[25] In Italy, Irene Brin noted the unbridled enthusiasm for Crawford's look:

> There was a Crawford style, a Crawford club, millions of Crawford
> fans, there was, above all, a Crawford mouth, with the upper lip in
> the shape of a kidney sausage and lower one like a slice of watermelon
> ... women workers poured out of offices at the end of the day, firmly
> convinced that they looked like her and, like her, deserved a villa with
> a swimming pool in California.[26]

In addition to Crawford's image, Adrian also created Greta Garbo's, turning her into an icon that thousands of women wanted to emulate. Soon after *A Woman of Affairs* was released in 1928, Garbo launched the trend for wearing cloche hats, while her plaid-lined trench coat, which was featured in *Women's Wear Daily*, inspired thousands of copies (pl.44).

The years that followed saw various types of hat come into fashion, such as the beret, thanks to *Ninotchka* (1939), or the turban, as worn by Garbo in *The Painted Veil* (1934). But her greatest influence on fashion was the pageboy haircut, which powerfully asserted the vogue for mid-length hair, just when *garçonne* hairstyles were the height of popularity. As Brin noted:

> She was the one who solved the hair problem. Our childhoods,
> surrounded by mothers with shaved necks and older sisters with Eton-
> style cuts, were filled with concerned questions and fearful sentences:
> 'Hair looks good very short or very long, what will we do when it
> starts to grow back? It must be either the *garçonne* or plaits, nothing

44
Greta Garbo dressed by Adrian in the film *A Woman of Affairs*, 1928

is worse than a mid-length style.' Instead the mid-length was a triumph and the pageboy cut lives on today, even twelve years later.[27]

While Adrian created looks for Joan Crawford and Greta Garbo, it was Travis Banton, head of costume at Paramount from 1927 to 1938, who created Marlene Dietrich's famous masculine suits. This look was much loved by film stars and a source of inspiration for many designers, from Yves Saint Laurent, a memorable re-interpreter of the tuxedo for women, to Giorgio Armani.

Italian films typically offered surrogates for these legendary figures and tried, unsuccessfully, to popularize particular fashions or styles. Most of the commercially available films at that time were known as *telefoni bianchi* (white telephone) films, a reference to the decor of films starring actresses like Garbo and Jean Harlow. *Telefoni bianchi* films were usually more popular, with provincial settings and dramas involving love stories and lottery wins. *Grandi magazzini* (Camerini, 1939) and *La Contessa di Parma* (Blasetti, 1937) are just two examples. The latter is particularly noteworthy in terms of the national identity of fashion, as it is set in an atelier and features the romantic intrigues of a model and a football player, from one fashion show to the next. The slight plot aside, it is interesting to note that the whole film is marked by a sense of the ridiculousness of the fashion world and the contrast between the French and Italian languages. The lead actresses, Elisa Cegani and Maria Denis, were dressed by the dressmaker Mary Matté[28] and the furriers Viscardi,[29] both based in Turin, with clothes provided by Italy's National Fashion Body.

Even period costume films, so popular in Hollywood in the 1930s, had a profound influence on Italian fashions of the decade. In November 1934, *Lidel* published an article entitled *L'influenza del cinematografo sulla moda* (Cinema's

Influence on Fashion) which praised two designs by the fashion house Tortonese, inspired by costumes worn by Greta Garbo in *Queen Christina* (1933). As the captions pointed out, in these designs 'the grandeur of costumes from the past merges with an intelligent understanding of the practical necessities of today, and these two dresses have their own noble and severe grace that many ladies will find persuasive'.[30] Similarly, an article in *Dea* in October 1936 patriotically noted that the costumes worn by Norma Shearer and Leslie Howard in George Cukor's *Romeo and Juliet* (1936) had been hand-embroidered in imitation of sixteenth-century Italian dress and made using Mariano Fortuny's Venetian textiles. 'This news is further proof of the admiration held for our wonderful artistic traditions,' the article concluded. 'It is easy to imagine a movement in international fashion inspired by our historical dress styles.'

Elsa Schiaparelli: Art is Fashionable

'What I do is taken up and copied by everyone,' said Coco Chanel. 'What I create is inimitable,' replied Elsa Schiaparelli (pl.45). 'Dress designing, incidentally, is to me not a profession but an art. I found that it was a most difficult and unsatisfying art, because as soon as a dress is born it has already become a thing of the past,' she continued. 'A dress cannot just hang like a painting on the wall, or like a book remain intact and live a long and sheltered life.'[31]

With her eccentric style, in some ways the opposite of the sober and minimal look of her bitter rival Chanel, who called her *l'italienne*, Schiaparelli was the 'other' protagonist of international fashion in the 1930s. Her pieces have been a source of inspiration for many in the fashion industry, from the aforementioned Adrian to Yves Saint Laurent, who paid tribute to Schiaparelli in his Autumn/Winter 1980 collection, and from Giorgio Armani, who dedicated his first haute couture collection (Privé) in Spring/Summer 2005 to her, to Dolce & Gabbana, John Galliano and Alexander McQueen.

Schiaparelli was born in Rome on 10 September 1890, into a family of intellectuals from the Piedmont region. Her father was an orientalist who translated works by Arabic poets and writers, and her cousin, Ernesto Schiaparelli, founded the Egyptian Museum in Turin. Schiaparelli seems to have been born with a sense of extravagance and profound irony. As she relates in her autobiography, written alternately in the first and third persons, one day she tired of her mother making her feel ugly, so she 'thought up ways of beautifying herself':

> To have a face covered with flowers like a heavenly garden would indeed be a wonderful thing! And if she could make flowers sprout all over her face, she would be the only woman of her kind in the whole world. Nasturtiums, daisies, morning glories, all in full bloom! With some difficulty she obtained seeds from the gardener and these she planted in her throat, ears, and mouth. She felt they ought to grow faster on her warm body than in the soil outside. Thus she sat waiting for the result. Alas, in this matter-of-fact world, the result was merely to make Schiap suffocate! Her mother, in a panic, sent for a doctor to remove all these dreams and illusions from her far too imaginative daughter.[32]

The Origins of Italian Fashion

Schiaparelli grew up in the Palazzo Corsini in Rome. On a visit to England in 1913, she met Count Wilhelm de Wendt Kerlor, whom she married the following year. After a brief period in London, the couple moved to Nice when World War I broke out. In 1919, they headed to New York. A fellow passenger on their ship was Gabrielle Picabia, the wife of artist Francis Picabia. A great friendship blossomed between the two women and Gabrielle introduced Schiaparelli to the avant-garde New York circle that included Marcel Duchamp and Man Ray. Schiaparelli shared their sense of humour and extravagance. Her relationship with her husband was not a particularly happy one, either emotionally or financially. So Schiaparelli began to work as a translator and in commerce, and was hired by the fashion designer Nicole Groult, Paul Poiret's sister, as a clothes saleswoman. Around the same time she separated from her husband, having found out about his affair with the dancer Isadora Duncan. In 1922, urged by friends such as Blanche Hays and Gabrielle Picabia, Schiaparelli moved to Paris with her daughter, Gogo. She immediately became part of French high society. Unlike Chanel and Vionnet, who were initially excluded because of their humble origins, Schiap – as she became known – had no difficulty in becoming integrated in the elite, thanks to her name and international education. In Paris, she met Paul Poiret:

> One day I accompanied a rich American friend to the small house bursting with colour which Paul Poiret had in the Rue St Honoré. It was my first visit to a *maison de couture* ... I put on a coat of large, loose cut that could have been made today ... 'Why don't you buy it, mademoiselle? It might have been made for you' ... 'I cannot buy it,' I said. 'It is certainly too expensive, and when could I wear it?' 'Don't worry about money,' said Poiret, 'and you could wear anything anywhere.' The compliment and the gift overwhelmed me.[33]

Not long after, Schiaparelli decided to dedicate herself to fashion: 'Once or twice I had thought that instead of painting or sculpture, both of which I did fairly well, I could invent dresses or costumes.'[34] Her sportswear debut took place at the same time, and international success came in 1927, when she opened an atelier called *Pour le sport* at 4 rue de la Paix: 'She arranged it to look like a boat, with ropes on which scarves, belts, and sweaters made a colourful disorder.'[35] That year Schiaparelli launched a range of sweaters, hand-knitted by Armenian women, with large *trompe-l'œil* bows on the front (pl.47). Apart from the New York department store Strauss, one of her first clients was Anita Loos, then at the height of her career thanks to the success of her book *Gentlemen Prefer Blondes* (1925). After the success of the first sweaters with bows, Schiaparelli created dozens of new designs, with seafaring tattoos, pierced hearts and X-ray or skeleton motifs. In 1929, Schiaparelli went back to the United States for the first time since 1922, staying for three weeks to present her latest sportswear collection at Stewart & Company. She was accompanied by her great friend Countess Gabriella di Robilant, who was helping her as a model and assistant. Soon afterwards di Robilant followed Schiaparelli's example and opened her own atelier in Milan called Gabriellasport.[36]

The Italian press paid close attention to Schiaparelli's career. In 1932, for example, the illustrator Mario Vigolo described her in *Moda* as 'the great Italian

artist', praising her 'happy finds' and her experiments with fabrics.[37] Capitalizing on her growing success, Schiaparelli opened a London branch of her atelier in 1933 and in the following year she launched no fewer than three perfumes. In 1935 she relocated to larger premises at 21 Place Vendôme. Her most devoted clients included Gloria Guinness, the Duchess of Windsor, Greta Garbo and Katharine Hepburn. During these years, Schiaparelli's natural affinity with the art world became increasingly evident and she began her collaborations with Jean Cocteau, Christian Bérard, Léonor Fini and Salvador Dalí. Together with Dalí she created jackets with lips for pockets, black velvet bags in the shape of telephones with embroidered gold dials, organza evening gowns decorated with enormous lobsters and some of her most famous hats, including one shaped like a shoe (pl.46).

Her costume jewellery, created in collaboration with Jean Schlumberger and artists including Elsa Triolet and Jean Clement, featured beetles, dragonflies and even aspirin tablets. Schiaparelli was also the first designer to centre her collections on a single theme and to turn her catwalk shows into genuine spectacles, anticipating two features that would later become routine. For Spring/ Summer 1935 she presented the *Stop, Look and Listen* collection, characterized by high-tech materials such as rhodophane, which she used to create astonishing clothes with a 'glass effect'. In the autumn of that year she used zippers to decorate sumptuous evening dresses. Her *Papillons* (Butterflies) collection of 1937 was followed by a circus-themed collection in 1938 (pl.48):

> Clowns, elephants, horses, decorated the prints with the words *'Attention à la Peinture'*. Balloons for bags, spats for gloves, ice-cream cones for hats, and trained Vasling dogs and mischievous monkeys ... The typical tempo of the time was marked by great enthusiasm. There was no criticism of 'Who can wear it?' As an amazing fact, Schiap did not lose a single one of her wealthy conservative old-fashioned clients but got a lot of new ones – and, of course, all the stars.[38]

48
Elsa Schiaparelli
Jacket from the *Circus*
collection (detail), silk twill
France, 1938
V&A: T.395&A-1974

The circus theme would later be reprised by many other designers: Alexander McQueen explored it in his Autumn/Winter 2001 collection, as did John Galliano for Christian Dior in 2003.

In 1939 Schiaparelli launched Shocking, a perfume in a bottle shaped like a female torso, designed by Léonor Fini. The bottle was inspired by the figure of Mae West, whom Schiaparelli had just dressed for A. Edward Sutherland's film *Every Day's a Holiday* (1937).

> To find the name of a perfume is a very difficult problem because every word in the dictionary seems to be registered. The colour flashed in front of my eyes. Bright, impossible, impudent, becoming, life-giving, like all the light and the birds and the fish in the world put together, a colour of China and Peru but not of the West – a shocking colour, pure and undiluted. So I called the perfume 'Shocking'.[39]

Femme Fatale or Perfect Housewife?

At the outbreak of World War II, shortly after the launch of her *Cash and Carry* collection, which featured garments covered in pockets for women who wanted to carry everything with them without needing a handbag, Schiaparelli moved to New York. In 1945, she returned to Paris, where she continued to run her atelier until 1954. In the same year she published her autobiography, *Shocking Life*, a reference to her predilection for shocking pink. Future talents such as Pierre Cardin and Hubert de Givenchy cut their teeth working in her atelier. Schiaparelli died in Paris on 13 November 1973, at the age of 83. Shortly before her death she sold her brand name, still active in perfumes and licensing today, to the Sassoli de' Bianchi family. In 2006 it was acquired by the Italian entrepreneur Diego Della Valle, who in 2013, after a haute couture capsule collection designed by Christian Lacroix, entrusted the artistic direction to Marco Zanini.

Gabriella di Robilant: Sportswear Pioneer

If Elsa Schiaparelli dominated the international fashion scene between the two world wars, her friend Gabriella di Robilant (1900–99), who founded the label Gabriellasport in 1932, was one of the pioneers of Italian sportswear. A member of the de Bosdari family, Gabriella was born in Florence in 1900. She moved to Venice in 1920 after her marriage to Andrea di Robilant, sole heir to the great Mocenigo fortune. In Venice, which Paul Morand described as the 'most brilliant city in Europe', Gabriella di Robilant embarked upon a dream life. When she was not receiving visitors at the Palazzo Mocenigo, she spent long days on the beach at the Lido, where she was part of a refined social circle that included Cole Porter ('His hands flew across the keyboard and accompanied his music with such beautiful words so full of real life that he made each one his own.'), the waspish American journalist Elsa Maxwell ('She invented public relations. She knew how to take advantage of the nouveau riche's mania for publicity. She knew its financial value. She was a diabolical being.'), the little-loved Gabriele D'Annunzio ('A horrible little bald man with a little pointed beard, who posed as a fawn and followed the young women with meaningful glances, both lascivious and cunning.') and Jean Patou ('To be original we raced to invite him.') (pls 37, 49–51).[40]

Patou, together with Chanel, was one of the leading exponents of the growing fashion for sportswear and he influenced Gabriella's decision to focus on this area. She wrote in her autobiography *Una gran bella vita* (1988): 'From Chanel and Patou I learned the science of clothing, I refined my taste, and later in their Paris ateliers I learnt many secrets of that art, which at the time was the prerogative of the French.'[41]

Apart from Chanel and Patou, Elsa Schiaparelli was also a major influence on Gabriella. Although, rather curiously, Gabriella does not mention her in her autobiography, Schiaparelli remembers her several times as a dear friend, recalling that when Gabriella lived in Paris for a time in the mid-1920s, 'we decided to share the flat'. Schiaparelli continued:

> At first all we could find were two nasty rooms in the Rue de Ponthieu, but later we found a very nice apartment in the Boulevard St Germain which suited us perfectly because it was in two separate

49
Group photo, c.1926
Andrea di Robilant, with his
arms around Cole Porter; behind
them Linda Porter, Elsa Maxwell,
Gabriella di Robilant, Fulco di
Verdura and Hollywood actor
George Sanders
Nicolis di Robilant Archive

50 *overleaf*
Group photo at the Venice
Lido, c.1928
Prince Cito, Bice Frigerio,
Mario Pansa, Gabriella di Robilant,
Charlie Besteigui, Lalia Yturbe,
Serge Lifar, Nathalie Paley
Lelong, Paola Medici del Vascello,
Count Bebino Salina, Lillia Ralli,
Count Andrea di Robilant
(left to right)
Nicolis di Robilant Archive

parts. We communicated with each other by telephone, never going
into each other's flat without first announcing ourselves. Thus we
preserved our friendship and, at the same time, we did not feel alone.[42]

Gabriella introduced her friend to many Parisian salons ('My friend Gab knew
many amusing people. She was gay and always busy and she helped me greatly
to get out of the too-retired life.'[43]). Later, when Gabriella experienced
difficulties, Schiaparelli took her on to work in her own atelier.

In the early 1930s, after Gabriella had separated from her husband, she
began to commission simple dresses from Venetian seamstresses. Both practical
and sporty, they were a far cry from the haute couture gowns made by the
traditional ateliers. In 1931 she was invited to present her designs at Nicky's, a
famous perfume shop on via Manzoni. They were so successful that she decided
to open an atelier on via Santo Spirito in Milan the following year. It was an
instant hit.

Along with the leading figures of Milanese high society, Mussolini's
daughter Edda Ciano also came to the atelier whenever she visited Milan. Gabriella
achieved international fame when Bergdorf Goodman, that temple of New York
luxury, invited her to present her designs in the States. In 1941 Gabriella moved
to Rome, where she took over the headquarters of the famous dressmakers
Ventura, the official supplier to the House of Savoy, at 93 Piazza di Spagna.[44]

Femme Fatale or Perfect Housewife?

51
Gabriella di Robilant with Fulco
di Verdura, c.1930
Nicolis di Robilant Archive

Madame Anna, who had been the director of the old atelier, continued to work in the new fashion house. Gabriella di Robilant described her as follows:

> She was a very small woman, hoisted up on orthopaedic heels, always dressed in black with a three-strand Majorca pearl necklace. Her hair was white and arranged fashionably, high on her head and caught in a fine black net that fell from the back of a little drum-shaped hat. She was born in Holland and said she was eighty years old.[45]

Madame Anna counted all the most important members of Roman nobility among her devoted clients. From then on, sportswear ceased to be the hallmark of Gabriellasport. The atelier started to create haute couture garments, often buying patterns from the most famous fashion houses, following the tradition established by Ventura.

> When it was time to prepare the patterns for the new season, Madame Anna closed herself in a room and organized the great manoeuvres like a general ... The floor was completely covered with shiny mountains of laminates, soft velvets, fine silks ... rivers of satin were thrown on the floor, printed silks, vicuna, luxurious Eastern cashmere. Occasionally the models fainted. When that happened work had to stop and Madame Anna shouted complaints that sounded like rolls of thunder. I was exhausted. I thought about the suppliers' bills and tried to reign her in. I forgave her because she was a great artist ... During the catwalk shows she stayed hidden behind the stage and only emerged to take the applause at the end.[46]

Madame Anna was very snobbish; if her clients lacked class she called them *smoscette* (droopy little girls) and generally charged them more than her aristocratic clients. Princess Isabella Colonna, who had helped her in difficult times, was one of her favourite customers. Gabriella di Robilant recalled that 'she would have given her the company'.[47] Madame Anna also loved Ninon Belmonte, Princess Torlonia and Laetitia Boncompagni Ludovisi. Gabriellasport continued to trade during the war, even when Madame Anna, who was of Jewish-Dutch origins, had to stop working, a victim of the Italian racial laws. After the war, the atelier experienced one of its happiest periods:

> Madame Anna could live without fear again and became even more authoritative than ever. But she also began to make magnificent clothes for the new stars of Roman society ... Mothers, lovers, and friends of the Allies arrived. The most brilliant period of the atelier began and [it] did great business.[48]

Soon there were new names in Roman fashion, who attracted members of the visiting international jet set. In 1948, after her second marriage, to the Sicilian nobleman Francesco Starrabba di Giardinelli, Gabriella moved to Palermo. It became increasingly difficult for her to follow the fortunes of the atelier, which remained under the direction of Madame Anna. A further problem lay in the fact that although Madame Anna was brilliant at her work, she paid

Femme Fatale or Perfect Housewife?

no attention to finances, as Gabriella found out to her cost: 'Hidden under mountains of fabric, she took a leap in the dark and gave it her all. She cut, sewed, created surprises and was about to ruin me.'[49]

In order to avoid bankruptcy, Gabriella sacked Madame Anna in 1948 and replaced her with the very able Ferdinando Sarmi, but he did not last long, leaving soon after to design for Elizabeth Arden in New York. In 1952, after being invited by Jordan Marsh to present her designs at the Sheraton Hotel in Boston,[50] Gabriella closed the atelier, tired of commuting between Rome and Sicily. Her decision caused an uproar. The seamstresses reacted angrily, protesting and demonstrating with slogans such as 'We have been thrown on to the streets', 'They have taken away our food' and 'We were the girls of the Piazza di Spagna'.[51] The latter was a reference to *Le Ragazze di Piazza di Spagna*, a bittersweet film by Luciano Emmer about the fashion world, which starred a splendid Lucia Bosé and had been shot in part on location at the Gabriellasport atelier the previous year.

Sport: A Burning Issue

The Fascist regime's contradictory stance towards women, on the one hand advocating the ideal of a woman confined to domesticity and on the other the benefits of a social education gained in the outside world, was highlighted in the 1930s through the question of sport (pl.53). This issue brought to light a profound difference between the female role models put forward by the Catholic Church and the regime. Unlike the Church, the regime encouraged women's physical development through competitions and races. Sportswomen often featured in the pages of various women's magazines; female figures who skied, sailed, swam or played tennis were heavily promoted, as were images of gymnastics and competitive sports involving girls belonging to Fascist organizations. *La Donna*, for example, had a column on gymnastics, while a 1939 issue of *Dea* included the following lines:

> Who could deny that sporting culture, seen as a means of perfecting beauty, strength, courage and willpower, is useful and should be increasingly encouraged among women? Naturally, a woman should also cultivate her maternal instincts; but if she is to be strong for motherhood, she must also possess a pleasing grace and we now know that with perseverance and the help of hygiene and sport it is possible to achieve surprising improvements in physical appearance.[52]

Fashion illustrations started to celebrate the sporting woman. In 1938, for example, the cover of the magazine *Signorina grandi firme* showed a hearty young woman, drawn by Gino Boccasile, wearing an elegant ski suit.

In the other camp, the Catholic Church linked physical activity with sterility, while the regime suggested that women's attempts at emancipation were the cause of the low Italian birth rate – on this point at least both sides were in agreement. Led by *Famiglia Cristiana*, the Catholic press declared itself to be anti-sport, condemning it as one of the principal enemies of the family and of women: 'Libertarianism, impiety, disorder, press immorality, depraved habits, the insatiable nature of industry that draws women into the workings of the factory,

Antiflex

P·M
S. A.
DOTT. PAOLO DE MEDICI

MANIFATTURA PELLI
PER PELLICCERIA

MILANO

53
ENIT (National Tourism Agency)
Poster advertising Cortina
d'Ampezzo, *Bellezza* 1941

the frivolity of fashion, which attracts women out of the home with amusements and sport.'[53]

Although women's sport was increasingly becoming a mass phenomenon, poorer and more deprived women, including those living and working in rural areas and those who had received little formal education, were still excluded.[54] By contrast, in middle-class and aristocratic circles sport became a prominent trend. Society events started to encompass sporting ones, such as the sailing regattas at Santa Margherita or San Remo, horse races, or skiing competitions at Cervinia or Sestrière. The appeal of this style was wide-ranging, from members of the royal family to well-known actresses to the family of Il Duce – Maria José loved skiing, while Edda Ciano preferred swimming and horse-riding. Indeed, Mussolini's wife was the only one of her family who did not share their passion for sport, preferring instead domestic and rural activities – like the chicken coop she had installed at Villa Torlonia that she personally looked after.[55]

Cortina d'Ampezzo

SPORT INVERNALI

PASSATE LE VOSTRE VACANZE SULLE MONTAGNE ITALIANE!

Dall'arco maestoso delle Alpi fino agli Abruzzi, fino all'Etna, le cui nevi contrastano con l'eterna primavera della Sicilia, una serie di alberghi e di rifugi è pronta ad accogliere gli appassionati della montagna con l'ospitalità più cordiale

INFORMAZIONI: ENTE PROVINCIALE PER IL TURISMO, AZIENDE DI SOGGIORNO E TUTTI GLI UFFICI VIAGGI

4

Self-Sufficiency

The National Fashion Body

In December 1932, the regime established the *Ente autonomo per la mostra permanente nazionale della moda* (Autonomous Body for the Permanent National Fashion Exhibition) in Turin. The capital of the Piedmont region was chosen for a number of reasons: it was the seat of the House of Savoy as well as a significant industrial city and it had a long history of fashion and elegance, due in part to its relative proximity to the French capital.

The new organization was set up[1] with the aim of nationalizing the complete fashion production cycle, from the planning stages through to packaging, with a national exhibition to be held twice a year in Turin, in the spring and autumn.[2] The first exhibition in April 1933 revealed the organization's innumerable shortcomings (pl.56). April was too late to present summer fashions – the clothes should have been shown in February at the latest, which would have allowed the smaller seamstresses to buy the patterns for the summer collections. Similarly, the winter collections needed to be presented in August rather than October.[3] Another problem was the lack of adequate infrastructure across the creative, industrial and commercial sectors.[4]

In order to establish a distinct Italian fashion, structures for appropriate professional training, particularly in fashion design, needed to be put in place. France provided an excellent example in this respect with its *École des Beaux-Arts* in Paris and the Chamber of Commerce in Lyon.[5] Although attempts were made to solve these problems in Italy, Lydia de Liguoro noted: 'Our dressmakers and modistes keep on running to Paris every six months or more to find out the new trends.'[6] With few exceptions, therefore, France still remained the arbiter of international fashion.

In the second half of 1935, against the backdrop of the Italo-Ethiopian war, the battle for self-sufficiency was central to every aspect of Fascist political economy, including fashion. On 31 October 1935 a law (no. 1293) was passed to change the constitution of the Autonomous Body for the Permanent National Fashion Exhibition and rename it the *Ente nazionale della moda* or National Fashion Body.

Designed to promote the progressive establishment of Italian fashion, the new organization enjoyed huge power right from the start. To understand the privileges it held, it is sufficient to examine some of the articles of the Royal Decree-Law of 26 June 1936, the *Disciplina della produzione e riproduzione di modelli di vestiario e accessori per l'abbigliamento* (Law on the production and

54
Silk bathing costume
Bellezza, May 1941

FERRARIO

Abito da pomeriggio in
moerro guarnito in volpi
argentate.

Disegno originale
di Mario Vigolo

reproduction of clothing designs and clothing accessories). The first article reads: 'Whoever prepares or presents their clients with collections or samples of clothing designs is obliged to declare their activities to the National Fashion Body.' This law, amended on 18 January 1937 (no. 666), enabled the Body to create a list of about 300 Italian dressmakers. It stipulated that all the enrolled firms were obliged to label at least 25 per cent of their products with a 'mark of guarantee' that certified the Italian provenance of their design and production (pl.57). As well as sending a photograph and fabric sample of each design to the Body, at their own expense, the firms had to pay a fee for each garment that was awarded the mark. The extremely complicated mechanism of this 'mark of guarantee' soon created countless problems, calling into question the ability of the Body's representatives to judge designs on the basis of photographic evidence alone. Furthermore, the 'mark of guarantee' was soon devalued because too

Self-Sufficiency

many were awarded: around 4,000 designs from the 1936 summer collections alone bore the mark.

Ester Lombardo, editor of *Vita femminile*, did not hold back in her criticisms of the new Body:

> In the first place, nearly 300 firms are too many in Italy. We do not know for sure how many designs there are bearing the mark but at least several hundred. It is true that they represent only 25 per cent of the creations of every firm, but even so this is too much ... Alongside the dresses and hats of important ateliers we can find the little hats from retail shops and off-the-peg dresses produced by the dozen, so that a lady can be dressed to look almost like her own cook, all in the name of Italy. This is a sacrifice we should not ask of any lady.[7]

In order to solve this problem, Lombardo suggested creating another kind of 'mark of guarantee' in order to distinguish haute couture ateliers from the smaller dressmakers. This was the first small step towards the future 'gold mark'. Another of the Body's failures was the lack of Italian fashion photographs available for publication in women's magazines and the fashion press, leading Lombardo to ask:

> Will the Body tell us who is going to supply us with Italian material in order to content our readers? Apart from a few photographs, not always of good quality, of the catwalk shows, the Body has nothing to give us. Despite this, it is ready to criticize us if we publish one of the French designs that the public enjoy looking at in all the newspapers they can easily find, large and small, which invade Italy from across the Alps. Where do the dressmakers get their ideas – I am talking about the smaller seamstresses – if not through French newspapers?[8]

In 1938, the problem of fashion photography generated a bitter argument between Lombardo and Roberto Farinacci, editor of *Critica Fascista*, a daily newspaper published in Cremona. He accused Lombardo of having published French-designed clothing in *Vita femminile* in February 1938. On 5 February, Farinacci published an article entitled *Cocciutaggine femminile* (Female Pig-headedness):

> Lombardo dedicates numerous pages to French fashion ... so is she not at all interested in the problem of autonomy raised by the Duce? And has she not realized that the entire Italian press is careful not to publish French designs? We think that an authoritative rebuke would put even our comrade back on to the right path. Perhaps without meaning to she is inciting our women to send our money to France, with a thoughtless contempt for Italian prestige, intelligence and economy.[9]

This article resulted in the issue of *Vita femminile* in question being withdrawn from newsagents. In the following issue, Lombardo responded to Farinacci's accusations:

Dear Farinacci, perhaps you are ignorant of the fact that there are no Italian fashion photographs fit for publication. Italian tailors and dressmakers take photographs to send to the Fashion Body for consideration for its mark. The Body cannot send the newspapers and magazines these photographs without betraying the professional secrets of the firms whose designs are not yet for sale. Conclusion: an Italian magazine might receive a few photographs, generally of poor quality, two or three times a year, at the seasonal presentation of the collections. For the rest, it has to purchase images from agencies, foreign ones it should be noted, who import the photographs that we pay for.[10]

Boycotting a country like France, which was innovative in the field of fashion both from a technical and an organizational point of view, was counterproductive. Instead, Italy should have taken its lead from France, providing the press with photo shoots of models and fashion houses. This did not take place, however, because it would have been illegal for the Body to reveal professional secrets by distributing the photographs they received from ateliers in order to receive the 'mark of guarantee'.

Among the initiatives proposed by the Body, it is worth noting the 1936 publication of the *Commentario Dizionario Italiano della Moda*, a fashion dictionary edited by Cesare Meano. Following the patriotic campaign to promote 'healthy Italian voices' launched by the Fascist regime, the fashion terms in this new dictionary were all Italianized and any foreign expressions still in use were eradicated.[11] So a suit was changed from a *tailleur* to a *completo a giacca* (set with jacket), a cardigan from *golf* to *panciotto a maglia* (knitted jumper), trousers from *pantaloni* to *calzone*, spots from *pois* to *pallini*, sequins from *paillette* to *pagliuzze*, a tuxedo from *lo smoking* to *giacchetta da sera* (evening jacket), flounces from French *volants* to Italian *volanti*. Satin became *raso*, silhouette became *figurina*, and so on. Leafing through fashion magazines printed shortly after the dictionary was published reveals a general move towards Italianization. Lucio Ridenti noted:

Anyone who, like me, has to spend time in fashion workshops – which dressmakers still call ateliers ... – will have heard the head dressmaker say phrases of this kind: Signora, do not worry, the *aplomb* of the dress will be fixed, we will enlarge the *bouffant* and adjust the *bordure*. As for the fur decorations, you can choose between the *breitschwanz*, the *petit gris*, or perhaps the *renard* or *rat musqué* ... all of which means, for someone who speaks Italian, that a woman does not think her long dress falls well and that her puffed sleeves are too small. Finally, she would like to choose fur decorations either in Persian lamb, grey squirrel, fox or musk rat.[12]

At this time, fur was highly promoted, with many different types proposed for all seasons, but it was always of Italian origin or at least from within the Empire. Fur was used not only for coats and cloaks, but also for stoles, neckwear and scarves, to the extent that it was rare to see a jacket, overcoat or dress in a fashion magazine without at least some kind of fur embellishment (pls 55, 71). Without exception, Italian designers continued to offer fur even in the summer.

For example, the summer collections of 1938 depicted in *La Donna* featured boleros of silver fox and ermine, as well as moleskin capes. Even if Italian furs were promoted most heavily, foreign furs were still being imported at the end of the 1930s.[13] Fur production processes became more innovative, as shown in the report for 1940 produced by the National Fashion Body. Sheepskin was treated to look like beaver, rabbit was dyed to resemble leopard, otter or Persian cat. The skins of squirrels, cats and even mice were used. A 1939 issue of *Per Voi Signora* included an article entitled *Pellicce di topo colorato* (Furs of Coloured Mice), all about the kinds of crossbreeding and diets that would produce the brightest coloured furs.

60
Salvatore Ferragamo with
a young apprentice, 1940s
Museo Salvatore Ferragamo

Salvatore Ferragamo: 'Shoemaker of Dreams'

In 1939, *L'Illustrazione Italiana* commented that Salvatore Ferragamo had
'succeeded in creating a new fashion, which did not exist before, that of female
footwear, bringing him international fame'[14] (pl.60). Writing about Italy's period
of self-sufficiency, Natalia Aspesi pointed out that 'it was Ferragamo, with his
orthopaedic sole, who invented the only authentic fashion of those years, the
only long-lived novelty, a symbol of those times'.[15]

   The eleventh of fourteen siblings, Salvatore Ferragamo was born into a
modest family in 1898 in Bonito, a village about 100 kilometres outside Naples.
Having served as an apprentice under shoemaker Luigi Festa at a very young
age, Ferragamo emigrated to the United States when he was 14. In the early
1920s, he set up his own business making and repairing shoes in Santa Barbara,
California. He first started working in the film industry during this period. In
1923 he moved to Los Angeles, where he opened the Hollywood Boot Shop.
Some of the most famous film stars of the time started coming to him, such as
Douglas Fairbanks, John Barrymore, Mary Pickford, Pola Negri, Joan Crawford
(pl.63) and Gloria Swanson. Ferragamo's first famous client, as he recalled in his
autobiography *The Shoemaker of Dreams*, was Lottie Pickford:

> It was for her that I created my 'First' model: a plain pair of court
> shoes in brown kidskin leather ... with twin 'ears' sticking up at
> the front ... After Lottie came Mary Pickford, whose feet were the
> prettiest, the best-shaped, and the smallest of all the many film stars
> I have shod.[16]

61
Salvatore Ferragamo
Woman's platform sandal with
sole composed of coloured
suedes covering cork
Italy, 1938
V&A: T.84-1988

62
Salvatore Ferragamo
Antelope suede lace-up shoe
with a prow-shaped toe
Italy, 1930-5
V&A: T.86-1988

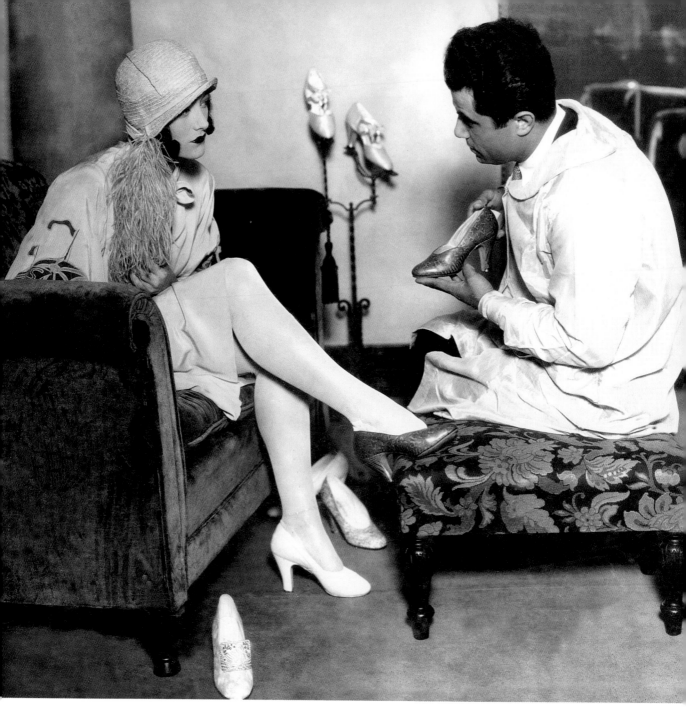

63
Salvatore Ferragamo with
Joan Crawford, c.1925
Museo Salvatore Ferragamo

For Gloria Swanson he made 'corkscrew heels, studded with imitation pearls', for Dolores Del Rio, 'rainbow-coloured evening shoes with ankle straps and tall gold heels' and for Lillian Gish 'multi-coloured satin slippers'.[17]

In 1927 Ferragamo returned to Italy and opened an atelier making bespoke shoes in Florence. Narrowly avoiding bankruptcy after the Wall Street Crash, he reached the height of his fame in the late 1930s thanks to that orthopaedic shoe with a cork sole (pl.61). The first client he showed this design to was the Duchess Visconti di Modrone. She was horrified but Ferragamo did not give up, telling her: 'Just let me make a pair for you … and wear them once. If you are not complimented on them bring them back, and we will forget all about it.'[18] So the Duchess allowed herself to be convinced and one day she

The Origins of Italian Fashion

wore the shoes to Mass. 'When I opened my salon next day they came to me in a continuous stream,' Ferragamo recalled. 'Within weeks the wedgie had become my most popular style. Every woman who wore it came to me to extol its comfort. The comfort was in the cork. Rubber would have given a jerky, springy step: cork makes the feet feel as if they are riding on a cushion.'[19] Thus Irene Brin noted: 'Industrious cobblers are breaking off Louis XV spool heels to replace them with 15 centimetres of cork ... wedges did not take long to conquer first the shop windows and then streets, houses and beaches, marking an imperious revolution in taste and a strange metamorphosis in proportions.'[20]

The Fashion Body did not hold back in its praise for the great shoemaker, whose business was not diminished by the atmosphere of emergency caused by the increasing lack of raw materials. Instead, the situation merely stimulated Ferragamo 'to use more disparate raw materials, from which he obtained noble elements to construct his designs, which are real jewels of elegant practicality. Cellophane, self-sufficient fibres, cork, textiles woven by hand by skilled rural housewives, all passed through the maker's hands like a crucible of transformation and perfection.'[21] At that time, as Ferragamo recalled:

> Mussolini came to me with corns and callouses; his mistress, Claretta Petacci, came to me. Eva Braun, Hitler's mistress, came, surrounded by Nazi guards; one morning four queens sat at the same time in the four corners of my Rome salon – the Queens of Yugoslavia, Greece, Spain, and the Belgians. The Maharani of Cooch Behar ordered a hundred pairs of my shoes.[22]

Apart from the wedge, another iconic Ferragamo design dating from this period was the 'invisible' sandal with a transparent upper, which won him a Neiman Marcus Fashion Award in 1947. Over the course of his career Ferragamo learnt the secrets of nearly every 'famous foot', from the perfection of Marlene Dietrich's – 'surely the possessor of the most beautiful legs, ankles, and feet in the world' – to Audrey Hepburn's long, narrow feet.[23] By 1950, Ferragamo's company had around 700 employees, and the first partial mechanization of his shoe production dates back to this period. When Ferragamo died in 1960, he left his wife Wanda and eldest daughter at the helm of the company. The only one of his six children to join the business, Fiamma Ferragamo (1941–98) was responsible for the design, production and sales of women's shoes as well as the company's leather accessories up until the year of her death. In the early 1960s, the birth and establishment of ready-to-wear, together with rising labour costs, meant that artisanal and bespoke products fell from favour. Consequently, the company gradually began to substitute manual labour with mechanical processes and to diversify its product range, creating accessories as well as clothing for men and women. In 1967, Fiamma Ferragamo won the Neiman Marcus Fashion Award, exactly twenty years after her father. In 1978, she created the popular 'Vara' model with its distinctive grosgrain bow, considered one of the brand's classic shoes. She also had the idea for the famous *gancino* or metal clasp that is used as decoration on Ferragamo shoes, bags and clothing. To this day, the company is still entirely family-owned.

Over time, the company has broadened its activities to include other sectors, from clothing and accessories to perfumes, transforming itself into a

64
Clothes made from
self-sufficient textiles,
1935-9

global luxury brand.[24] In 1995 the Ferragamo Museum opened at the Palazzo Spini Feroni in Florence with an archive of over 10,000 footwear designs and a small collection of eighteenth- and nineteenth-century shoes as well as clothing and accessories. Apart from displaying a rotating selection of shoes, the museum also organizes and promotes exhibitions, conferences and events dedicated to fashion and contemporary culture.

Self-Sufficient Textiles

The textile industry played an important role within the panorama of self-sufficient fashion. Italian manufacturing decreased significantly after the crash of 1929, and the textile industry was one of the sectors hardest hit by the Depression. While the highest losses were experienced in the cotton and silk industries, the production of artificial fibres increased greatly.[25] This was an area that had begun to develop in Italy after World War I. In 1916, the Artificial Silk Society was founded in Padua and, with a number of other companies, went on to form the Cisa-Viscosa Group. In 1919, the company SNIA, with around two hundred million lire in capital, began to concentrate on the production of synthetic fibres.[26] Twenty years later, SNIA-Viscosa took over the Cisa-Viscosa Group, becoming the primary Italian and European producer of synthetic fibres.

For the textile industry, raw materials were a delicate issue: although Italy could achieve self-sufficiency in terms of silk, linen and hemp production, cotton, jute and wool were a different matter. The structure of the Italian textile industry was completely transformed by the chemical industry, which pushed synthetic fibres on to the market.[27] As self-sufficiency became more important, this area was promoted even further (pl.64). In 1935, there was a shift in Fascist economic policy, as Mussolini underlined:

> 18 November 1935 is already a date that marks the beginning
> of a new phase in the history of Italy. 18 November brings with
> it something definitive, I would like to say irreparable. The new
> phase of Italian history will be dominated by this premise: to realize
> as quickly as possible the greatest self-sufficiency in the Nation's
> economic life ... No Nation can achieve economic autonomy in
> the absolute sense, in other words 100 per cent; and, even if it were
> possible, it probably would not be useful. But every Nation tries to
> free itself as much as possible from enslavement to other countries.[28]

Faced with a shortage of raw materials, the regime announced several new directives, making it obligatory to blend a certain percentage of artificial fibres in with natural fibres that could not be produced domestically, as was the case with cotton and wool. Following these directives, the proportion of natural fibres used in wool dropped from 48 per cent in 1934 to 33 per cent in 1939, with the remaining amount composed of alternative fibres.[29]

The public had a certain mistrust of synthetic fibres, despite their being officially promoted. In 1939, Pietro Merli, head of public relations at the textile company De Angeli-Frua, declared that it was necessary to improve the image of these materials:

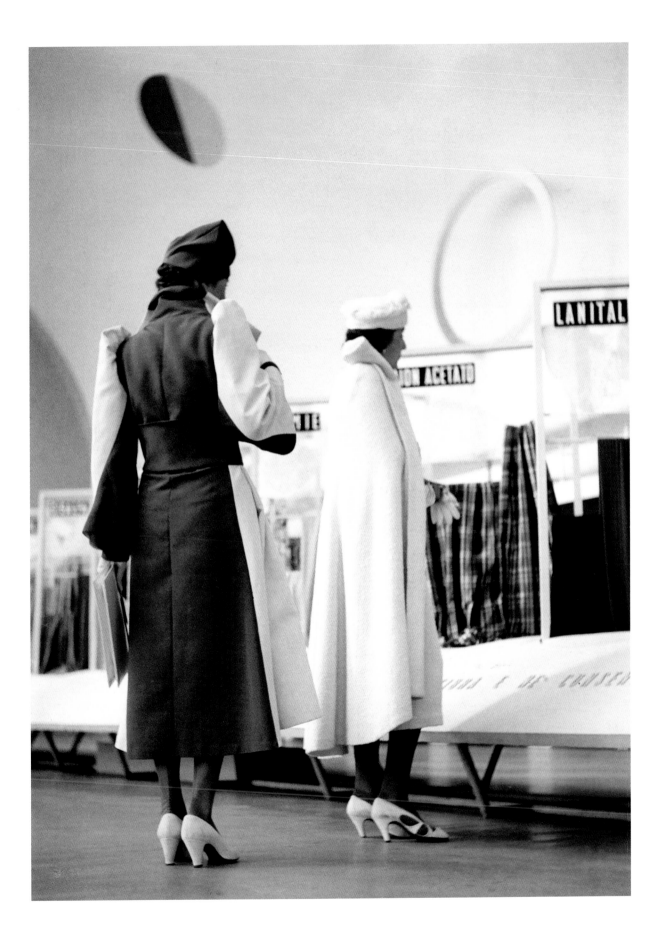

The concept behind an effective campaign of this kind is the following: to assert that synthetic fibres and the textiles made from them are a 'logical product of progress'. Even primitive populations use pure cotton and pure wool, but we are a civilized population belonging to a new, futuristic, mechanized civilization.[30]

'Self-sufficient textiles' included rayon[31] and its derivatives as well as lanital, cisalfa, broom, ramie, Spanish grass, mulberry, orbace and angora (pl.65). In 1935, when sanctions were imposed during the Italo-Ethiopian war, SNIA-Viscosa acquired the Italian patent for lanital, a new synthetic fibre derived from casein, invented by the chemist Antonio Ferretti.[32] While SNIA-Viscosa had lanital, Cisa-Viscosa developed and put on the market cisalfa, another synthetic wool substitute. Lanital's success was short-lived, however. When the markets reopened and, above all, as more sophisticated fibres were developed, casein-based fibres ceased to be used in Italy or the other countries that had followed its example.[33]

Broom is worthy of special mention among these self-sufficient fibres. In his speech to the second assembly of the guilds in 1937, Mussolini said: 'Broom ... which grows spontaneously everywhere, was known to many Italians only because Leopardi dedicated one of his most touching poems to it: now it is a textile fibre that can be exploited industrially.' Broom was generally used in its pure state or blended with other fibres as a substitute for cotton or jute.[34] Orbace was also of particular importance: the regime chose this rough Sardinian wool for winter uniforms. It was promoted as being particularly durable, as well as humidity- and waterproof.[35]

'The imagination that seems to be missing in the literary field has instead found an important outlet in the art of textiles', *Dea* commented in the face of such a variety of fabrics. 'Indeed, all the most unthinkable combinations of textile fibres have been devised to create the richest quality of fabrics.'[36] The introduction of rayon – 'the most modern of Italian textiles and the most Italian of modern textiles' – led to a revolution in women's clothing.[37] Initially used for knitwear and stockings, until the 1920s the fibre still had a major drawback: if a single thread broke, the damage soon spread across the whole garment, with disastrous results.[38] As time passed, significant advances were made so that rayon became run-resistant and more durable.

During these years, the Italian clothing industry made increasing use of rayon in its different forms – including viscose, acetate and flock – either on its own or mixed with wool, cotton or silk. Around 1930, rayon made up about 50 per cent of the total consumption of silk factories.[39] One great innovation was the invention of a matt version: until this point, rayon's shininess meant that its use was restricted to luxury goods.[40] In Italy, factories in Turin were the first to begin experimenting with the new textile in 1905, followed by factories in Padua and Pavia.[41] Production kept increasing, and in 1925 Italy became the second-largest producer of rayon in the world, behind the United States, maintaining this position until it was pushed into third place by Japan in 1932. However, Italy remained the biggest exporter of rayon in the world for many years.[42] In his book *Le arti d'oggi*, Roberto Papini praised the scientific progress of the Italian textile industry, with at times excessive enthusiasm:

65
Luisa Spagnoli
Angora sweater, *Rassegna
dell'Ente nazionale della
moda*, 15-31 May 1939
Biblioteca Nazionale
Centrale, Rome

Chemistry and physics have endowed textiles with new riches …
Velvets as light as crêpes, damasks as soft as veils … and mixes of
natural matt silks and very shiny artificial silks … the most bizarre
hybrids, damasked crêpes and velvet tulles and brocaded gauzes and
satin mesh, in millions of shades and tones so that even Iris would be
amazed to see them if she reappeared. … And Sandro Botticelli, who
wove his Madonna and angels and Primavera with flowing fabrics,
using dreamlike threads and golden embroideries, would fall to his
knees and make the sign of the cross.[43]

5

Fashion in Wartime

Fashion on the Eve of War

Towards the end of the 1930s, the activities of the National Fashion Body became increasingly insistent. On 16 June 1939, a law came into force that outlined the 'gold mark' for designs produced by haute couture houses, among other things. The introduction of the mark, which was only applied from 1941 onwards, did not produce the desired effect: in the first two sessions, 678 patterns presented by 31 clothing companies were examined, out of which 142 were granted the mark.[1] Yet most of the fashion houses – from Ventura to Zecca,[2] from Montorsi to Ferrario and Calabri – continued to 'draw inspiration' from French fashion, reproducing outfits from the Parisian catwalks with minor adjustments. The large ateliers could afford to send representatives to the Paris shows to buy patterns, while the smaller dressmakers employed the services of patternmakers who attended the shows twice a year to purchase designs they could sell back in Italy. The most famous of these was Rina Pedrini, known professionally as Rina Modelli. Maria Pezzi wrote that at the Paris shows 'the Italian companies and her colleagues spied on [Modelli], they watched her because they knew she had an infallible eye. When she was interested in a dress, she pretended to nod off, to sleep, to try and put the others on the wrong track. She bought 250 patterns each season.'[3] Shops selling paper patterns were very popular at this time, and one of the most prestigious ones was Casa Line in Rome, vividly described by Irene Brin:

> We need a dress, but we don't know how to sew, and it seems that our dressmaker doesn't either. She makes grand gestures in the air, brandishes her scissors, then stops and starts to talk about Turin, where she learnt her profession ... Our dressmaker tells us that 'to make a truly elegant dress, an exclusive, tailored design' is a simple thing. You just need to go to Rome, at the start of via Nazionale, in a big shop called Casa Line and buy a paper pattern ... What a street via Nazionale is! You can really find everything there ... We immediately spot the windows of Casa Line, which are low and covered with spectres of tissue paper. When you go into the shop the spectres become hundreds ... Around the ghosts, there are many women with rather glowing faces ... you could see servants with shopping bags, and young ladies with grey hats. Then there was a group of old-fashioned ladies, the kind that wear a little white silk ribbon around their

66
Ventura
Beach outfit,
Bellezza, June 1941

67–70
Moro
Outfit in crêpe *albene*
(a type of artificial silk),
Bellezza, May 1941

neck, and there were also baronesses, widows of important officials
… If the baronesses are boring, the servants are ideal clients. They
choose dresses in flowery fabrics, possibly with flourishes and drapes,
something complicated, they faithfully listen to the rather disdainful
advice of the dressmakers, they buy and then leave happy.[4]

One of the initiatives organized to promote Italian fashion was the
Exhibition of Self-Sufficient Clothing, which opened in Turin on 12 May 1940,
a month before Italy entered World War II. A number of different fashion houses
took part, including Biki, Fercioni,[5] Ventura and the Botti sisters.[6] Judging by
the descriptions of their designs, it is clear that fur was still very much in fashion
– most afternoon and evening clothes were trimmed with fox fur. Irene Brin
noted that society conversations often revolved around furs: 'I can't get the fox,
I will get the fox, I got the fox, were the successive stages of all female greed.'[7]
Alongside fur and the aforementioned fashion for cork wedges, there was a
growing trend for turbans, which was inspired by Hollywood stars from Greta
Garbo, who wore one in *The Painted Veil* (1934), to Joan Crawford, who wore a
gold lamé turban in her role as the cunning, husband-stealing perfume-counter
girl in *The Women* (1939).

This exhibition of self-sufficient fashion was due to close with the
Congresso nazionale dell'abbigliamento e dell'autarchia (National Congress on
Clothing and Self-Sufficiency), to be held on 8 and 9 June 1940. But, given
the highly volatile political climate created by the war, the event never took
place. During the course of its preparation, no fewer than 130 speakers had been
assembled. Their papers were to address a variety of issues, from the structure
of the clothing industry and technical challenges – including the publication
of adequate measurements or the use of standard sizing, the presentation of
samples and the preparation of designs and photographs – to legal problems,
such as how to protect designs from being copied.[8] One of the issues raised in the
proposals submitted to the congress was that of the excessive concessions of the
'mark of guarantee'. Vittorio Montano, owner of Ventura, was among those who
addressed this problem:

> In the opinion of those who know, this application has exceeded
> its limits and the intentions of those who proposed it. It is almost
> obligatory to award the mark to all the designs presented, as long as
> they are made from Italian textiles and they are not banal copies of
> foreign patterns.[9]

The figures presented in the official report for that year, the *Relazione del
presidente sull'attività svolta nel 1940*, confirm Montano's observation. Out of
the 14,074 designs presented to the Body in 1940, which included clothes, hats
and furs, no fewer than 13,889 received the 'mark of guarantee'. The Body's
inspectors carried out only 364 inspections in order to stamp out the copying
of designs, identifying 128 contraventions and giving 18 cautions.[10] Another
problem highlighted by the report was the precarious state of serial production,
due not only to the lack of an efficient chain of department stores but also to
people's strong attachment to made-to-measure clothing, fostered by the large
numbers of skilled dressmakers in Italy.[11]

Fashion During World War II

When German troops occupied Paris in 1940, the fashion universe suddenly lost its centre. The international capital of style was cut off from the world for four years, and so it was no longer possible to depend on France for innovations. During the war, the governments of English-speaking countries intervened in the fashion industries; Britain launched the Utility Clothing Scheme in 1943, using the slogan 'Fewer, simpler, better' to encourage the adoption of more versatile and economic clothing.[12] New clothes were rationed in June 1941, with a points system based on the amount of material used and the number of hours required to make the garment. The British government issued each person with a ration book of 48 coupons per year. A coat required 18 points. The CC41 mark, for

'Civilian Clothing 1941', soon became a guarantee of quality. Clothing carrying this symbol was made by the Incorporated Society of London Fashion Designers, to which designers such as Norman Hartnell and Hardy Amies belonged. In the United States, the government applied restrictions to aid war production in 1943. Known as Regulation L85, they were more moderate than the system of rationing in Britain. While the Allies rolled out a form of wartime socialism, in Italy the regime tried to minimize any difficulties. The newspaper *Il Popolo d'Italia* wrote:

> We need to develop and support fashion and the activities connected with it, even at this time when the Italian people's lifestyle has become more austere. Although women's clothing purchases must be contained in proportion to the changing situation, they must not be abandoned, and they should not be considered as evidence of a lack of sensitivity toward greater and more important problems.[13]

Newspapers continued to run the usual features on gowns to wear to balls and the theatre, on elegant hats and furs, just as they had done before. It was only at the end of 1941, as the war worsened, that the regime also introduced a system of rationing cards and points for clothing. The November 1941 issue of *Bellezza* included an article entitled *Risorse della moda secondo le discipline dell'abbigliamento* (Fashion Resources in Clothing) (pl.75):

> War fashion ... Rationing cards. Points. About ten years ago, or a little more, chronic economic problems abroad provoked

72
Cerri, dress; De Senibus, hat, *Bellezza*, May 1942

73
Ensemble by Zecca, *Rassegna dell'Ente nazionale della moda*, 15-31 July 1939 Biblioteca Nazionale Centrale, Rome

74
Federico Pallavicini
Illustration for gaiters made
by Gegia Bronzini from leftover
wool and other fabrics,
Bellezza, September 1942

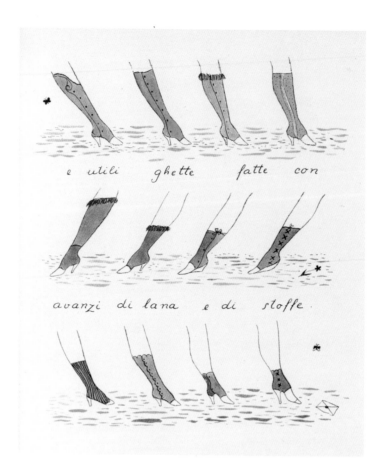

e utili   ghette   fatte   con

avanzi   di   lana   e   di   stoffe.

an extreme financial crisis across the whole world, forcing people
to economize ... If necessary, muffs could be transformed into little
bags. Reversible dresses or cloaks could be worn to show one side or
the other ... The reversible cloak and dress will reappear, renewing
the easy miracle of an apparent multiplication of clothing. And
then the game of details and accessories (belts, little collars, cuffs,
bibs, and so on), which will greatly extend this game of illusions
with the help of imagination and patience. But fashion, beyond this
transformative capacity, will also have the benefit of other resources,
as we have already described.[14]

Only hats were excluded from rationing: 'Hats will not be affected
by rationing: you can have as many as you like'[15] (pls 72, 76). The rationing
system functioned like this: every citizen had a points card and each garment
was worth a certain number of points. There were five types of card, the values
of which varied according to age and sex. A shirt was worth five points and a
pair of pyjamas eight. There were three types of coupon, marked either with
Roman numerals, Arabic numerals or letters of the alphabet. Coupons with
Arabic numerals were used to buy clothing and accessories, Roman numerals
for underwear and domestic textiles and letters of the alphabet for haberdashery.
The coupons were valid for a year, and to avoid people spending them all at
once, the regime announced that a certain number of points had to be used
every three months.[16]

75
Brunetta
Illustration for *Bellezza*,
September 1941

Italian women were thus forced to review their wardrobes. Hems
started to skim the knees again, and there was a new trend for fitted jackets
with padded shoulders, which seemed to echo military uniforms. One of the
most popular outfits of the time was the *tailleur* (woman's suit), or *abito a
giacca* as it was then called. Depending on the event or time of day, it could be
customized with accessories. 'The *abito a giacca* can be used for all occasions,
simply change the shirt. Classic shirts, blouses in shiny satin or opaque crêpe
can all take turns,' *Bellezza* suggested. 'Let's not forget knitted jumpers. How
beautiful the ones made of rabbit angora are!'[17] Silk stockings disappeared, to
be replaced with special make-up for legs or gaiters made from leftover wool
(pl.74). Irene Brin wrote:

> In France at the moment women are wearing extraordinary tulle hats
> on top of old, worn-out clothing, and they do not have stockings but

Fashion in Wartime

76
Lila de Nobili
Illustration for a hat
by Gauturon,
Bellezza, June 1941

77 *opposite*
Brunetta
Illustration for *Bellezza*,
May 1941

a make-up for legs, they do not have real shoes but slippers lined with
leather. In England it has been officially announced that there will be
no silk stockings until after the war. In Germany there are shoes with
straw soles, made by prisoners.[18]

Because of the lack of textiles, skirts became shorter during the war, and
the Church's attitude towards women also became increasingly severe. This
was partly because women were wearing fewer garments, compensating for
the textile shortage, but also because of an increasing desire among women for
emancipation. In an allocution for young Catholic girls on 22 May 1941, Pope
Pius XII bitterly deplored women's fashions. The same year, the Catholic Church

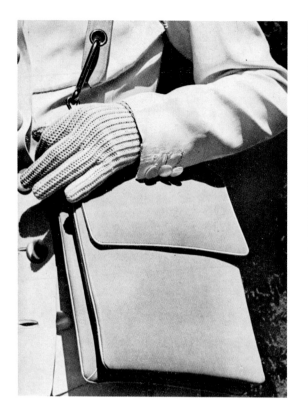

and the regime proposed a campaign to abolish women's trousers, with the excuse that they were 'imported garments, which generally deprive women of their delicacy and female grace'.[19]

Women compensated for austerity in clothing with strong make-up and elaborate hairdos, as well as extravagant accessories. 'We will have shiny hair, not with brillantine, but from endless brushing, which will make up for less washing because of the lack of water. We will have skin smooth from a pumice stone, if we have to give up soap,' wrote *Bellezza*. 'Regret for distant beaches will melt away and a taste for fresh dwellings among courtyards and gardens, green and flowery balconies, will be revived.'[20] At the same time, *Dea* launched a regular feature on fashion in wartime, which addressed a different theme every month, starting with recycling. Suggestions were offered, such as how to alter old clothes found at the back of the wardrobe, or how to transform bedcovers and curtains into garments. As in the past, war certainly spurred on creativity: we have only to remember that one of the most famous dresses in cinema history – the green velvet gown worn by Scarlett O'Hara (Vivien Leigh) in a memorable scene from *Gone with the Wind* (1939) – was made from a curtain because of shortages during the American Civil War. Similarly, given that it was impossible to import patterns from France during World War II, authentically Italian, British and American fashions began to develop. A new generation of designers flourished in Britain and the United States, including Norman Hartnell, Charles James and Claire McCardell. At the same time, besides Ferragamo, Italy saw the emergence of talents such as Gucci, Prada, Fendi and Fratti.

Gucci was founded in Florence by Guccio Gucci (pl.79).[21] After having worked as a lift-boy at the Savoy Hotel in London, Gucci began an apprenticeship with the Franzi company in Milan.[22] Returning to Florence, he opened his first workshop of saddlery and travel goods on via della Vigna Nuova in 1921. In 1938 he opened a branch on via Condotti in Rome. In the years of self-sufficiency, faced with the shortage of raw materials, Gucci distinguished itself by the use of materials hitherto considered unusual in the leather industry, such as hemp, jute and especially bamboo, which became a distinctive symbol of the label, along with the double 'G' logo.

Meanwhile, in Rome Fendi was establishing itself, having been founded as a leather and fur workshop on via del Plebiscito in 1925 by Edoardo and Adele Fendi (pl.82),[23] while in Milan Prada, a leather goods company founded in 1913 by the brothers Mario and Martino Prada (pl.81), had been a supplier to the House of Savoy since 1919 (pl.80).[24] During World War II, Prada became known for its luggage in featherweight fustian, described by Elsa Robiola in *Bellezza* as 'extremely light valises (a few ounces) without a frame, so that they can be folded like an item of clothing … They are so well made, with details and handles in leather, that they will not compromise – rather they will enhance – the appearance of elegant lady travellers.'[25]

Described by Maria Pezzi, doyenne of Italian fashion, as 'the king of mad jewellery', Giuliano Fratti made buttons, clasps, decorations and trinkets in cheap materials such as cork, raffia, string and straw combined with stones. Born into a family of textile manufacturers, he started working at a very young age, making fabric labels for dressmakers. Having made contact with a number of fashion houses, he decided to embark on a career making accessories and costume jewellery, encouraged by the dressmaker Giuseppina Tizzoni. 'My fortune lay in

going against the prevailing trend. I made false jewels when women only wore
real ones,' Fratti recalled. 'I always made belts even when women were only
wearing shift dresses. And the beauty was that I always sold them. My friends
used to say: "If it's made by Fratti it's in, even if it's ugly."'[26]

Combined with a historic tradition of highly skilled craftsmanship, this
climate of burgeoning Italian creativity came to full fruition after the war. If
the inconsistency of the National Fashion Body had the effect of suffocating
many initiatives, we must also acknowledge its various merits. Thanks to this
organization, the entire fashion production system in Italy became regulated.
Interviewed in the 1990s, Biki, one of the protagonists of the early years of
Italian fashion, recalled: 'There were stirrings, attempts based mainly on the use
of Italian textiles, our passementerie, lace and embroidery made by our extremely

The Origins of Italian Fashion

skilled artisans. But, despite their efforts, it lacked competency and unity of intentions. It did not have a proper joined-up strategy.'[27]

Immediately after the war, France desperately needed to win back its old clients in Europe and the United States. In order to do so, it organized the *Théâtre de la Mode*, an exhibition designed to demonstrate the continuing vitality of French fashion. The idea was a very old one: that of sending fashion dolls around the world to publicize the latest trends. After they were presented in Paris on 27 March 1945, the dolls went on a tour that visited London, Vienna, Stockholm, Barcelona, Copenhagen and a number of American cities. Maria Pezzi recalled that there were '200 wire dolls, the descendants of the "fashion dolls" of the seventeenth and eighteenth centuries, the *piavole de Franza* (French dolls), as they were called by Venetian ladies, demonstrating to the world that haute couture was still alive'.[28]

In the meantime, thanks to the European Recovery Program, also known as the Marshall Plan after Secretary of State George Marshall, and Prime Minister Alcide de Gasperi's visit to the United States in 1947, Italy was transformed into a kind of American colony.[29] American women who landed at Capri became immersed in a dream that could be summed up in four words: 'Sun, sea, pizza, love'. The cost of living was very low, Latin lovers were irresistible. This beautiful country, with its architectural and natural wonders, feared no rivals. In the cinema, there was *Roman Holiday* (1953), directed by William Wyler, in which Audrey Hepburn, a princess on an official visit to Rome, is stunned by the beauty of the Eternal City, forgets all her responsibilities and puts herself in the hands of the charming Gregory Peck. Arriving in the capital, actresses, princesses and first ladies began to frequent the new fashion houses that had opened their shutters after the war in place of the traditional old guard represented by Zecca, Montorsi, Sorelle Botti, Aurora Battilocchi and Ventura. The new fashion houses bore the names of the Fontana sisters, Emilio Federico Schuberth, Roberto Capucci and Fernanda Gattinoni, as well as of numerous noblewomen like Simonetta Colonna di Cesarò and Giovanna Caracciolo di Avellino, founder of Carosa. Thanks to them – and to the initiative of Giovanni Battista Giorgini, who in the early 1950s had the idea for group fashion shows held at the Sala Bianca in the Palazzo Pitti – Italian style freed itself from centuries of French dominance and began its rise to international triumph.

Notes

Introduction
1 Quoted in De Liguoro, 1932
2 Founded in 1868, it was legally recognized in 1884 and modified in 1927.
3 Butazzi, 1980, p.25

Chapter 1
1 Levi Pisetzky, 1995, pp.50–1, ed. 1978
2 Ibid., p.23
3 See Roche, 1989, pp.468–70. The popularity of the *poupées de mode* began to decline with the rise of fashion magazines, which became the main channel for circulating information in the fashion sector. For more on this subject, see also Davanzo Poli, *Il sarto*, in Belfanti and Giusberti (eds.), 2003, pp.523–56.
4 Orsi Landini, Niccoli, 2005, p.26
5 Muzzarelli, 2011, p.46
6 Rose Bertin (1747–1813) was a *marchande de modes*. Diderot's *Encyclopédie* defined this term as referring to someone involved in 'the sale of everything relating to headwear and male and female ornaments', see Morini, 2010, pp.21–4. For more on Rose Bertin, see Sapori, 2003.
7 Sapori, 2003, p.41
8 Morini, 2010, p.31
9 Ibid., pp.30–3
10 Quoted in Golbin, 2003, p.57
11 Hollander, 1982, p.440
12 Quoted in Levi Pisetzky, 1969, p.338
13 Margherita, the first queen of Italy, exerted a powerful influence on fashion. Her clothing and comportment were frequently the source of great admiration. When she received a group of Milanese ladies in the Blue Room at the Royal Palace in Milan in 1870, she was described as wearing 'a very valuable headdress of emeralds, with an extremely magnificent pink gown decorated with white laces and frills'.
After she became queen, one of her greatest admirers was the republican poet Giosuè Carducci. In 1879 he wrote: 'The Queen is a beauty and very kind lady, who speaks very well and dresses splendidly.' At the same time, Margherita inspired his poem *Alla Regina d'Italia e il liuto e la lira*.
14 *Margherita*, 27 February 1887
15 Quoted in Morini, 2000
16 Italy had led dress fashions in the early Renaissance as well.
At the time, people referred to 'Italian-style' clothing, an implicit acknowledgment of a national concept of fashion (see M. Cataldi Gallo, *La corte come centro di diffusione della moda*, in G. Butazzi, R. Varese (eds), *Storia della moda* (Bologna, 1995), pp.58–60). See also Davanzo Poli in Belfanti, Giusberti, 2003, pp.523–60.
17 Quoted in Levi Pisetzky, 1995, p.86
18 Ibid., p.86
19 Levi Pisetzky, 1980, pp.97–108
20 Cambedda, Cardano, 1983, p.55
21 Quoted in Chesne Dauphiné Griffo, 1983, p.34
22 For more on Rosa Genoni see Fiorentini Capitani, 1996, *L'ornamento di pura arte italiana: la moda di Rosa Genoni*, in Various Authors, *Abiti in festa l'ornamento e la sartoria italiana*, pp.40–59.
23 In haute couture houses, the *première* transforms the designer's sketch into a cloth pattern or toile and fits it on the atelier's mannequin.
24 Quoted in Cambedda, Cardano, 1983, p.56
25 Minnini, 1991, p.61
26 *La Donna* was published from 1905 until 1968.
27 Quoted in Franchini, 2002, p.284
28 Garbini was in business from 1865 to 1901, when the company was acquired by the publishers Verri.
29 Between 1864 and 1867, the publisher Edoardo Sonzogno launched four women's periodicals dedicated to fashion.
30 The brothers Emilio and Giuseppe Treves were particularly active in the women's press from 1870 until Emilio's death in 1916, after which the publishing house began to decline. In 1938 it merged with Garzanti.
31 The same phenomenon occurred with catalogues for shops, such as Aux Villes d'Italie owned by the Bocconi brothers and the Mele department store, both offering the same dress designs at different price points for different sectors of the public. For example, in *Margherita*, on 1 April 1896 (vol. XVIII, no. 7) the same patterns could be purchased by mail order in paper (for 1.50 lire) or muslin (for 3 lire). For
more on this subject, see also Lazzi, 1983, *Moda: problemi e metodi per una ricerca* in *Galleria del Costume* I, pp.15–18.
32 Published by Garbini from 1866 until 1915, *Monitore della moda* was the Italian version of *Moniteur de la mode*. In Italy it was advertised as the 'newspaper that, without doubt, more than any other, can keep its female subscribers up-to-date with all the most beautiful and interesting novelties of Paris fashions', from *Il magazzino della damigella*, 1 March 1887, vol. XXXIV.
33 From 1891, the cost of subscribing to *Margherita*, which moved from a weekly publication to a fortnightly one, fell from 24 to 18 lire per year.
34 *Margherita*, 1 May 1900, no. 9
35 The magazine was published from 1888 until 1912.
36 *La Donna*, special double issue, 5 April 1909, no. 103, pp.22–3.
37 The woman's suit, or *tailleur*, first became popular at the end of the nineteenth century, making its debut in the Italian press in 1888, in the pages of *Margherita* (Levi Pisetzky, 1969, p.353). Epitomizing the taste for clothes suited to sporting or outdoor activities, this garment derived its name from the fact that it was made by a male tailor, or *tailleur*, rather than a female dressmaker, or *couturière*. Despite the name's French origins, the *tailleur* actually first appeared in England, where its creation has been attributed to John Redfern, tailor to Queen Victoria.
38 Quoted in Baroncini, 2010, p.114
39 The name came from the London store opened by Arthur Lasenby Liberty in 1874, specializing in textiles and objects in a floral style.
40 Praz, 2002, pp.1051–2
41 Quoted in Baroncini, 2010, p.69
42 Morini, 2000, p.135
43 Italian attitudes towards her proposals are reflected in *Viva il Bloomerismo*, a satirical poem by Arnaldo Fusinato published in *Corriere della Dame* in December 1851 and quoted in Aspesi, 1993, pp.126–30.
44 Gnoli, 2009b, p.7
45 Quoted in Davanzo Poli, 1992, p.51
46 Quoted in Romanelli, 1999, p.20
47 In 1922, Fortuny began a collaboration with the interior designer Elsie Lee McNeill, the future Countess Gozzi. After Fortuny's death, the Gozzi family continued to produce his textiles until 1998, when it sold the rights to Maged Riad. See Steele, 2005, volume II.
48 Quoted in Orsi Landini, 1999, p.472
49 Orsi Landini, 2000, pp.30–41
50 Tirelli, Vergani, 1981, p.103

Chapter 2
1 Norchi, 1919
2 Ricci, 1991, p.12
3 At the same time, there was a greater push for improved education for women. In 1919, the Sacchi law was approved, granting women a new series of rights. Similar laws had already been passed in 1840 in the United States and 1870 in Britain.
4 *La moda in tempo di guerra*, 1916, pp.74–5
5 'It' was that certain something halfway between personality and sex appeal, or even a kind of 'strange magnetism' capable of attracting both sexes, as Elinor Glyn herself described it.
6 Sohn, 1994, pp.112–13
7 Quoted in Gautier, 2011, p.64
8 Brin, 1981, pp.78–80
9 Jean Alexandre Patou (1880–1936) opened his first atelier in 1912. Between 1923 and 1932 he was one of the leading French *couturiers*. In the early 1920s he became one of the major exponents of sportswear, creating the look embodied by the French tennis player Suzanne Lenglen, an icon of sporting style. In 1924 he opened an atelier selling holiday fashions. Patou was the first *couturier* to use his monogram on his designs, and therefore the first to use a logo in the modern sense. In 1930, he launched his perfume Joy (created by Henry Alméras), which is still a classic among women's perfumes. He advertised it with a slogan devised by Elsa Maxwell: 'The most expensive perfume in the world.'
10 In the 1920s, French designer Madeleine Vionnet (1876–1975) had a clandestine presence in Rome, at 3 via Lucullo, run by Miss Iolanda Hellè Herronett. See Capalbo, 2012, p.99

11 Quoted in Kamitsis, 1997, p.4

12 Quoted in Gnoli, 2009c, pp.146–9

13 Albanese, 1918, p.11

14 Albanese, 1938, pp.12–13

15 Taken from the title of De Liguoro's book, *Le battaglie della moda* (Rome, 1934)

16 Albanese, 1938, p.7

17 Albanese, 1918, p.7

18 Albanese, 1938, p.7

19 De Liguoro, 1934, p.8

20 Ibid., p.7

21 A Milanese fashion house that was very successful between the wars.

22 An Italian fashion house founded in Milan in 1815 that became known for its ability to reproduce French designs. At the height of its success, it was named as the official supplier to the Royal Household and in 1923 it opened a branch in Rome. Ventura closed in the 1940s.

23 Created in 1923, as part of the National Fascist Federation of the Clothing Industries, with the aim of freeing Italian fashion from French domination. See Grandi, Vaccari, 2004, p.105

24 Grandi, Vaccari, 2004, p.107

25 The Bocconi stores were Italy's first department stores. In 1865, Ferdinando Bocconi, a travelling salesman of used clothing, opened a menswear shop in Milan. It was very successful and the store became Bocconi's first department store, Alle città d'Italia, also known as Aux Villes d'Italie. In 1877, Ferdinando and his brother Luigi founded Società Fratelli Bocconi, with branches in various Italian cities. By 1880, between 100 and 150 employees worked at each branch, while the two main stores in Milan and Turin employed a total of 900 people. In the late 1870s the Bocconi stores began to offer a mail order service, with the catalogue *Album delle novità stagionali*. For more on this subject see Piunti, 'Un circolo vizioso: industria dell'abbigliamento e distribuzione in Italia tra le due guerre' in Various Authors, *Per una storia della moda pronta* (Florence, 1991), pp.196–8 and Antonio Catricalà, 'Il catalogo Bocconi: vestirsi per corrispondenza a fine '800', in Catricalà (ed.), 2004, pp.133–58.

26 It is significant that, according to the Industrial Census of 1937–9, there was a total of 125 large distribution stores, compared with 500,000 traditional fixed shops and 250,000 travelling salespeople. The same census recorded that department stores accounted for only 1.1 per cent of total retail sales. See Piunti, (cited note 25), pp.196–9.

27 For more on the relationship between Futurism and fashion, see Enrico Crispolti, *Il futurismo e la moda* (Venice, 1986)

28 Orsi Landini, 1991, p.40

29 Crispolti, 1986, pp.89–91

30 Quoted in Crispolti, 1986, p.12

31 De La Haye, 1988, (Italian edition 1990, p.66)

32 Quoted in Uzzani, 2003, p.12

33 Crispolti, 1986, p.135

34 Thayaht, in *Oggi e Domani*, 1930

35 Quoted in Crispolti, 1986, p.137

36 Ibid., p.143

37 Ibid., p.144. The company was founded in Alessandria in 1857 by Giuseppe and Lazzaro Borsalino. In 1979, Teresio Urselli, the last heir of the Borsalino family, gave up the company. In the early 1990s the company was acquired by a group of entrepreneurs from Asti, and in recent years exports have been greatly increased.

38 Crispolti, 1982, p.147

39 Ibid., p.181

Chapter 3

1 *Alla moda italiana*, 1930, pp.19–21

2 Guida, 1930. John Guida (1888–1951) was an Italian illustrator with English origins. His name was changed to Gion in line with the campaign of Italianization launched by the regime in the 1930s.

3 Giovanni Montorsi (1883–1945) opened the atelier Montorsi in Rome in 1920. In the 1930s, the atelier on via Condotti became the obligatory destination for the regime's wives and lovers. At the height of its success, it had 100 employees. The atelier closed in the early 1960s.

4 For more on Fascist economic policy, see *Annali dell'economia italiana 1930–38* (Milan, 1983) and *L'economia italiana tra le due guerre* (Rome, 1984); Ciocca and Toniolo (eds), *L'economia italiana nel periodo fascista* (Bologna, 1975). For more on fashion in the Fascist era, see Gnoli, 2000.

5 De Liguoro, 1932

6 The initial funding for the Autonomous Body for the Permanent National Fashion Exhibition was supplied by the Provincial Council of the Financial Cooperative of Turin (300,000 lire); two banks, the Cassa di Risparmio of Turin (250,000 lire) and the Istituto San Paolo of Turin (150,000 lire); the Provincial Fascist Federation of Commerce of Turin (10,000 lire), the Fascist Industrial Union of Turin (200,000 lire), the Provincial Fascist Federation of Commerce of Turin (100,000 lire) and the Turin Society to Promote National Industry (2,000,000 lire). *Copie di deliberazioni Enti Finanziatori*, Central State Archives, Rome, Presidenza Consiglio Ministri (prov.), 1934–36. See S. Gnoli, 2000, *La donna, l'eleganza, il fascismo*, p.44. Law no. 1618, *Costituzione dell'Ente autonomo per la mostra permanente nazionale della moda in Torino*, published in the *Gazzetta Ufficiale*, 26 December 1932.

7 De Liguoro, 1932

8 From the title of Meldini's book, *Sposa e madre esemplare: Ideologia politica della donna e della famiglia durante il fascismo* (1975).

9 Brin, 1981, p.115

10 Quoted in Gnoli, 2000, p.45

11 Quoted in Various Authors, *Il pappagallo giallo* (1986), p.73

12 *Lidel* was published until 1935.

13 *Lidel*, 1932

14 Ibid.

15 Mondello, 1987, p.91

16 *Dea*, February 1935, p.3

17 Gnoli, 2000, pp.48–51

18 See also Chapter 4.

19 Cesarani, 1981, p.76

20 Longanesi, 1936, p.1134

21 With eight Oscars and over 30 nominations, American costume designer Edith Head (1897–1981) won more awards than any other costume designer in cinema history during her career spanning more than 50 years.

22 Quoted in La Vine, 1980, p.210

23 Quoted in McConathy, Vreeland, 1976, p.86

24 Johnny Weissmuller was famous for playing Tarzan in 11 films produced by MGM between 1932 and 1948.

25 Quoted in Chierichetti, 1976, p.17

26 Brin, 1981, p.95

27 Ibid., p.94

28 A famous Turin atelier with a branch in Rome. Between the 1930s and 1950s it was visited by the most elegant women of Turin.

29 A furrier founded in Turin in 1904, which closed in the early 1990s. The company was most successful between the 1930s and the 1960s.

30 'L'influenza del cinematografo sulla moda', *Lidel*, November 1934, p.37

31 A. Madsen, *Coco Chanel: una biografia*, in P. Colaiacomo and V.C. Caratozzolo, *La Londra dei Beatles* (Rome, 1996), p.139

32 Schiaparelli, 1954, p.6

33 Ibid., pp.38–9

34 Ibid., p.42

35 Ibid., p.49

36 Blum, 2004, p.15

37 Quoted in Lupano, Vaccari, 2009, p.251

38 Schiaparelli, 1954, pp.91–2

39 Ibid., p.89

40 Gnoli, 2009a, pp.114–20

41 Di Giardinelli, 1988, p.38

42 Schiaparelli, 1954, p.48

43 Ibid., p.50

44 Archivio G.B. Giorgini, 1951–52, 1a00374

45 di Giardinelli 1988, p.77

46 Ibid., pp.79–80

47 Ibid., p.80

48 Ibid., p.84

49 Ibid., p.90

50 She presented 120 garments, each one named after an Italian city.

51 Gnoli, 2009a, pp.114–20

52 *La donna, lo sport, la bellezza*, 1939, p.11

53 *Famiglia Cristiana*, 1939

54 Gnoli, 2000, pp.52–5

55 Isidori Frasca, 1983, p.128

Chapter 4

1 22 December 1932, Law no. 1618, Constitution of the Autonomous Body for the Permanent National Fashion Exhibition.

2 Ferracini, 1934–6

3 Vera, 1933, p.298

4 De Liguoro, 1933

5 De Liguoro, 1934, p.106

6 Ibid., p.107

7 Lombardo, 1936a, p.9

8 Lombardo, 1935, p.19

9 Quoted in Lombardo, 1938, pp.9–10

10 Ibid.

11 Meano, 1936, p.IX

12 Quoted in Aspesi, 1982, p.94

13 *Relazione del presidente sull'attività svolta durante l'anno 1940*, 1941, pp.69–70

14 *Salvatore Ferragamo e la moda delle calzature femminili*, 1939, p.973

15 Aspesi, 1985, p.9
16 Ferragamo, 1957, pp.55–6. The book was first published in 1957 in English and translated into Italian in 1971.
17 Ibid., p.92
18 Ibid., p.144
19 Ibid., p.145
20 Brin, 1981
21 *Documento moda*, 1942
22 Ferragamo, p.159
23 Ibid., p.204
24 In 2010 Massimiliano Giornetti was named artistic director of the label.
25 Minniti, 1984, pp. 304–05
26 Garofoli, 1991, p.33
27 Tremelloni, 1937, pp.175–6
28 Mussolini, 1937, p.XVIII
29 Butazzi, 1980, p.28
30 Merli, 1939, pp.20–1
31 A cellulose derivative, rayon looked like silk – although its appearance varied depending on the fibres it was combined with – and for a long time it was known as artificial silk. Unsurprisingly, this name sometimes caused confusion, and in 1933 a law was passed to stop man-made fibres being referred to as silk. From then on the fabric was called rayon in Italy, the name it was given by the American industrialist Kenneth Lloyd. In April 1936, however, the National Fascist Federation of Industrialists of Artificial Fibres unanimously agreed to call it *raion*, Italianizing the word by removing the foreign letter 'y'.
32 Gnoli, 2000, p.72
33 Garofoli, 1991, p.38
34 Pistolese, 1937, pp.278–92
35 Ribuoli, 1980, p.35
36 'Le fibre tessili', *Dea*, November 1937, p.43
37 *Natura*, March 1936, p.38
38 Garofoli, 1991, p.27
39 Ibid.
40 Ibid., p.28
41 *Prima mostra nazionale della moda*, 1933, p.90
42 Meano, 1936, p.370
43 Quoted in Fanelli, 1986, p.238

Chapter 5
1 *L'alta moda italiana nel quadro della nuova disciplina valorizzatrice: la 'marca d'oro'*, 1941, pp.24–5
2 Founded by Nicola Zecca in via Ludovisi, Rome. Between the 1930s and the 1950s, it was considered to be one of the best ateliers in the city, making cloth toiles of French brands. After the death of Zecca and his wife, their valuable archive was acquired by dressmakers Tirelli.
3 Vergani, 2009, pp.1003–04
4 Brin, 1938, pp.44–6
5 A Milanese fashion house founded in 1910 by Giovanni Fercioni. Initially specializing in menswear, it later concentrated on women's clothing and was particularly known for its wedding gowns. During his career Fercioni dressed many Italian celebrities, including actresses Marta Abba and Elsa Merlini. In 1960 he celebrated the fiftieth anniversary of the atelier with a large party. The atelier closed when he died.
6 A fashion house founded in 1911 by Augusta, Carlotta and Fernanda Botti. The sisters' first atelier was on via del Babuino in Rome; from 1927 the business was on via Mercadante. Their clients included Queen Elena, art historian and museum director Palma Bucarelli and actresses Isa Barzizza and Anna Magnani. The dressmakers continued to operate until the late 1970s, specializing in faithful reproductions of French designs.
7 Brin, 1981, p.85
8 *Relazione del presidente sull'attività svolta durante l'anno 1940*, 1941, pp.56–7
9 Montano, 1940, pp.135–42
10 *Relazione del presidente sull'attività svolta durante l'anno 1940*, 1941, pp.56–7
11 Ibid., pp.55–6
12 Quoted in Giordani Aragno, 1991, p.19
13 *Guerra e moda*, 1939, p.46
14 'Risorse della moda secondo la disciplina dell'abbigliamento', *Bellezza*, November 1941, pp.3–5
15 Ibid., p.5
16 'Il sistema della tessera o carta individuale dei punti', *Bellezza*, November 1941, p.37
17 'Consigli a tre amiche', *Bellezza*, January 1942, p.5
18 Brin, 1981, pp.88–9
19 Quoted in Butazzi, 1980, p.26
20 'Estate in città', *Bellezza*, June 1942, p.64
21 In addition to the handbag with the bamboo handle (1947), among Gucci's classics are: the loafer with the double ring and bar motif (1952–3); the 'Flora' scarf (1966); ribbons inspired by saddle girths and the logo with the double 'G'. Between 1989 and 1993 the Gucci family progressively ceded control of the company to the Anglo-Arab financiers Investcorp International, and after various other transitions Gucci was acquired by the PPR group (1999–2001). In the 1990s Domenico De Sole, managing director and president (1995–2004), and the Texan designer Tom Ford (1994–2004) managed the relaunch of the historic label. In 2005 artistic direction passed to Frida Giannini. In 2011, to celebrate its ninetieth anniversary, Gucci opened a museum in its native city.
22 A leather workshop founded in Milan in 1864.
23 In the 1960s the five daughters of the founders took over from their parents, and in 1965 they appointed the German designer Karl Lagerfeld artistic director. Together they revolutionized and updated the concept of fur. Over the years, in addition to fur, Fendi bolstered its leather goods and introduced ready-to-wear lines. In 1996 the label reached the height of its popularity with the 'Baguette' bag, conceived by Silvia Venturini Fendi. Between 1999 and 2004 the LVMH group (Louis Vuitton Möet Hennessy) became the majority shareholder.
24 In 1978 Miuccia Prada, granddaughter of Mario Prada, took over the lead of the company together with her husband, Patrizio Bertelli. From the 1990s Prada introduced a conceptual fashion based on simple and essential designs, transforming the label into one of the most emblematic of the early twenty-first century. Always interested in the arts, she opened the Fondazione Prada in 1995 with the intention of promoting international artists. She is famous for an experimental approach to fashion and for her continual experimentation with materials, which have won her widespread acclaim from the press and international critics. Her numerous aesthetic innovations have earned her prizes and recognition such as the International Award for Accessories (1993) and the International Award (2004) from the Council of Fashion Designers of America, as well as the Metropolitan Museum's Costume Institute exhibition 'Schiaparelli and Prada: Impossible Conversations' in 2012.
25 Elsa Robiola, '20 giorni di vacanze, 20 chili di bagaglio', *Bellezza*, July 1942, pp.44–7
26 Quoted in de Cesco, 1972, p.6. Until 1972, when the firm closed, Fratti collaborated with French and Italian dressmakers, including Battilocchi, Zecca, the Fontana sisters and Mila Schön.
27 Quoted in Vergani, 1992, p.34
28 Quoted in Chiavarone, 'Théâtre de la mode', in Vergani (ed.), *Dizionario della moda* (2010 Edition; Milan, 2009), p.1154
29 Bianchino, Quintavalle, 1989, pp.13–14

Bibliography

Adrian, 'La creazione della moda per lo schermo', in Mario Verdone (ed.), La moda e il costume nel film (Rome, 1950)

Fortunato Albanese, Il perchè del I Congresso Nazionale fra le industrie dell'abbigliamento (Rome, 1918)

Fortunato Albanese, Profili di un'opera e di un programma (Rome, 1938)

'Alla moda italiana', in La Donna, February 1930

'L'alta moda italiana nel quadro della nuova disciplina valorizzatrice: la "marca d'oro"', in Rassegna dell'Ente nazionale della moda, 20 June 1941

Natalia Aspesi, Il lusso e l'autarchia (Milan, 1982)

Natalia Aspesi, I protagonisti della moda. Salvatore Ferragamo (1898–1960) (Florence, 1985)

Natalia Aspesi (ed.), Storia della moda (Milan, 1993)

Maurizio Barberis, Claudio Franzini, Silvio Fuso, and Marco Tosa (eds), Mariano Fortuny (Venice, 1999)

Daniela Baroncini, La moda nella letteratura contemporanea (Milan and Turin, 2010)

François Baudot, Elsa Schiaparelli (Paris, 1998)

François Baudot, Mode du Siècle (Paris, 1999)

Cecil Beaton, The Glass of Fashion (London, 1955)

Carlo Marco Belfanti and Fabio Giusberti (eds), Storia d'Italia. Annali 19. La Moda (Turin, 2003)

Bellezza, January 1941

Gloria Bianchino, Arturo C. Quintavalle, Moda Italia 1951–1989. Dalla fiaba al design (Novara, 1989)

Dilys Blum, Elsa Schiaparelli (Paris, 2004)

N. Bocca, 'Il passato nella moda d'oggi', in Butazzi and Molfino (eds), 1992

Gabriele Borghini and Gianna Piantoni, Vestiti per immagini (Rome, 2003)

Rossana Bossaglia, Anna Braggion, and Marziano Guglielmetti, Dalla donna fatale alla donna emancipata (Nuoro, 1993)

Irene Brin, Usi e costumi. 1920–1940 (Palermo, 1981, second edition 1989)

Irene Brin, Dizionario del successo, dell'insuccesso e dei luoghi comuni (Palermo, 1986)

Grazietta Butazzi, 1922–1943. Vent'anni di moda italiana (Florence, 1980)

Grazietta Butazzi and Alessandra Mottola Molfino (eds), La moda e il revival (Novara, 1992)

Emma Calderini, Il costume popolare in Italia (Milan, 1934)

Anna Cambedda and Nicoletta Cardano, 'Appunti per in discorso di moda femminile in Italia', in Various Authors, Roma Capitale 1870–1911. I piaceri e i giorni: la moda (Venice, 1983)

Roberto Campari, Miti e Stelle del Cinema (Rome and Bari, 1985)

Cinzia Capalbo, Storia della moda a Roma. Sarti, culture e stili di una capitale dal 1871 a oggi (Rome, 2012)

Gian Paolo Cesarani, Vetrina del Ventennio 1923–1943 (Rome and Bari, 1981)

Federico Chabod, L'Italia contemporanea (1918–1948) (Turin, 1961)

Giuliana Chesne Dauphiné Griffo, 'Moda e costume a Roma capitale', in Various Authors, Roma Capitale 1870–1911. I piaceri e i giorni: la moda (Venice, 1983)

Caterina Chiarelli, Carlo Sisi, and Giovanna Tennirelli (eds), Le collezioni. L'abito e il volto. Storie del Costume dal XVIII al XX secolo, Galleria del Costume di Palazzo Pitti (Livorno, 2003)

Caterina Chiarelli (ed.), Moda femminile tra le due guerre (Livorno, 2000)

Caterina Chiarelli (ed.), Per il sole contro il sole Thayaht & Ram. La tuta/ modelli per tessuti (Livorno, 2003)

David Chierichetti, Hollywood Costume Design (London, 1976)

Pierluigi Ciocca and Gianni Toniolo, L'economia italiana nel periodo fascista (Bologna, 1975)

Quirino Conti, Mai il mondo saprà. Conversazioni sulla moda (Milan, 2005)

Enrico Crispolti, 'Svolgimenti del futurismo', in Various Authors, Anni Trenta. Arte e cultura in Italia (Milan, 1982)

Enrico Crispolti, Il futurismo e la moda (Venice, 1986)

Doretta Davanzo Poli, 'Fortuny e il suo ideale di classicità', in Butazzi and Molfino (eds), 1992

Fred Davis, Fashion, culture and identity (Chicago, 1992)

Dea, February 1935

L. De Angelis, La moda italiana negli anni Quaranta del Novecento, thesis, Bachelor of Science in Fashion and Costume, Università degli Studi La Sapienza, Rome, 2004–5

M. De Cesco, 'Addio Signor Bottone', Panorama, 10 August 1972

Victoria De Grazia, Consenso e cultura di massa nell'Italia fascista. L'organizzazione del dopolavoro (Rome and Bari, 1981)

Amy De la Haye, Fashion Source Book (London, 1988)

Lydia De Liguoro, 'Verso una moda italiana', Il Popolo d'Italia, 19 November 1932

Lydia De Liguoro, 'La moda italiana', Il Popolo d'Italia, 12 January 1933

Lydia De Liguoro, Le battaglie della moda 1919–1933 (Rome, 1934)

Documento Moda, Ente nazionale della moda (Turin, 1942)

'La donna, lo sport, la bellezza', Dea, July 1939, p.11.

Georges Duby and Michelle Perrot (eds), A History of Women in the West (Cambridge, MA, 1994)

'Estate in città', in Bellezza, June 1942, p.64.

Giovanni and Rosalia Fanelli, Il tessuto Art Decò e anni Trenta (Florence, 1986)

Oddone Fantini, La moda nei tempi e la moda fascista (Rome, 1929)

Silvio Ferracini, Programma di massima dell'Ente autonomo per la mostra permanente nazionale della moda, 16 February 1933, Central State Archives, Rome, Presidenza Consiglio Ministri (prov.) 1934–36

Salvatore Ferragamo, Shoemaker of Dreams (London, 1957)

'Le fibre tessili', Dea, November 1937, p.43

Silvia Franchini, Editori lettrici e stampa di moda (Milan, 2002)

Maura Garofoli, Le fibre intelligenti (Milan, 1991)

Jérôme Gautier, Chanel: Lessico della moda (Novara, 2011)

Gabriella di Giardinelli, Una gran bella vita (Milan, 1988)

Bonizza Giordani Aragno (ed.), Il Disegno dell'Alta Moda Italiana 1940–1970 I. Progetto e stile. Creatori della linea italiana (Rome, 1982)

Bonizza Giordani Aragno, 'Per una storia della moda in Italia', in Chiara Buss (ed.), Seta, il Novecento a Como, Fondazione Antonio Ratti (Milan, 2001)

Bonizza Giordani Aragno (ed.), Donne tra Brividi ed Emozioni (Rome, 2002)

Cristina Giorcelli (ed.), Abito e identità. Ricerche di storia letteraria e culturale, Vol. VII (Palermo and Rome, 2007)

C. Giorgetti, 'Firenze tra le due guerre. Un'anteprima sulla culla dell'Italian Style', Imago Moda, October 1990

Sofia Gnoli, 'La moda si tinge di nero', in Domitilla Calamai and Sofia Gnoli, Cento anni di stile sul grande schermo (Rome, 1995)

Sofia Gnoli, La donna, l'eleganza, il fascismo (Catania, 2000)

Sofia Gnoli, *Moda e cinema. La magia dell'abito sul grande schermo* (Città di Castello, 2002)

Sofia Gnoli, *Gran Sera. Dalla Hollywood sul Tevere agli anni Ottanta* (Rome, 2003)

Sofia Gnoli, *Adrian: Il glamour degli anni d'oro di Hollywood*, in Maria Catricalà (ed) *Per filo e per segno. Habitus in fabula* (Soveria Mannelli, 2006)

Sofia Gnoli, *Moda e teatro. Le creazioni per il palcoscenico di Poiret, Lucile, Chanel, Saint Laurent, Lacroix, Gaultier, Versace* (Rome, 2008)

Sofia Gnoli, 'Gabriella di Robilant. A Majestic life', supplement to issue 709, *Vogue Italia*, September 2009a, pp.114–20

Sofia Gnoli, 'Introduzione a Paul Poiret', in *Vestendo la bella epoque* (Milan, 2009b)

Sofia Gnoli, '*La couturière des déesses*', supplement to issue 703, *Vogue Italia*, March 2009c, pp.146–9

Sofia Gnoli, 'Camaleontica Irene Brin', *Velvet*, January 2011, p.60

Pamela Golbin, '*La haute couture est morte. Vive la haute couture*', in Quinto and Tinarelli (eds), 2003, pp.57–9

Silvia Grandi and Alessandra Vaccari, *Vestire il ventennio* (Bologna, 2004)

'Guerra e Moda', *Rassegna dell'Ente nazionale della moda*, 15–31 October 1939

John Guida, '*Moda di Regine, di Principesse, di Dame in occasione delle nozze dei Principi di Piemonte*, *Fantasie d'Italia*, February 1930, pp.14–15

Aristotile Guido, *Le industrie del vestiario e l'incremento delle fibre tessili nazionali*, Federazione Nazionale Fascista degli Industriali dell'Abbigliamento, 1936

Anne Hollander, *Seeing Through Clothes* (Los Angeles and London, 1978)

Anne Hollander, 'When Worth was King' (1982), in Welters and Lillethun (eds), 2011, pp.437–42

'Influenza del cinematografo sulla moda', *Lidel*, November 1934, p.667

Rosella Isidori Frasca, *E il duce le volle sportive* (Bologna, 1983)

Lydia Kamitsis, *Madeleine Vionnet* (Florence, 1997)

La Donna, special double issue, 5 April 1909

La Donna, special edition for the International Exposition in Turin, 1911

Venessa Lau, 'Heir Force One', *W*, March 2009, pp.198–202

W. Robert La Vine, *In A Glamorous Fashion* (London, 1980)

'Le nozze di Edda Mussolini', *La Donna*, May 1930

Rosita Levi Pisetzky, *Il costume e la moda nella società italiana*, vol. V (Milan, 1969)

Rosita Levi Pisetzky, *Il costume e la moda nella società italiana* (Turin, 1978, second edition 1995)

Rosita Levi Pisetzky, 'Il borghese e la moda', *Epoca*, 12 April 1980

Gilles Lipovetsky, *L'Empire de l'éphémère* (Paris, 1987)

Ester Lombardo, '*La Moda in Italia*', *Vita Femminile*, December 1935

Ester Lombardo, '*Il primo esperimento di moda italiana*', *Vita Femminile*, April 1936a

Ester Lombardo, '*La moda autunnale e il nuovo marchio dei modelli*', *Vita Femminile*, September 1936b

Ester Lombardo, '*Consuntivo di una polemica*', *Vita Femminile*, March 1938

Leo Longanesi, '*La donna 1937 cerca uno stile*', in *L'illustrazione italiana* (LXIII), 27 December 1936

Mario Lupano and Alessandra Vaccari (eds), *Una giornata moderna. Moda e stili nell'Italia fascista* (Bologna, 2009)

Margherita, no. 9, vol. XXII, 1 May 1900

Filippo Tommaso Marinetti, 'Contro il lusso femminile', *Roma Futurista*, 4 April 1920

Richard Martin, *Fashion and Surrealism* (New York, 1987, second edition 1996)

Richard Martin, *The St. James Fashion Encyclopedia: A Survey of Style from 1945 to the Present* (Detroit, 1997)

Dale McConathy and Diana Vreeland, *Hollywood Costume: Glamour! Glitter! Romance!* (New York, 1976)

Cesare Meano, *Commentario Dizionario Italiano della Moda*, Ente nazionale della moda (Turin, 1936)

Pietro Merli, '*Proposte: propaganda per i tessili artificiali*', in *Rassegna dell'Ente nazionale della moda*, 31 March 1939, pp.19–22

Elisabetta Merlo, *Moda italiana. Storia di un'industria dall'Ottocento a oggi* (Venice, 2003)

Massimo Minnini, '*Architettura e moda le "vetrine torinesi"*', in Various Authors, *1900–1960. L'alta moda capitale. Torino e le sartorie torinesi* (Milan, 1991)

Fortunato Minniti, '*L'industria tessile*', in Various Authors, *L'economia italiana tra le due guerre* (Rome, 1984)

'La moda in tempo di guerra', *Margherita*, 1 March 1916, pp.74–5

'Moda sul palcoscenico e sullo schermo', *Dea*, October 1936, p.33

Elisabetta Mondello, *La nuova italiana: la donna nella stampa e nella cultura del ventennio* (Rome, 1987)

Indro Montanelli, *Gli incontri*, (Milan, 1961, second edition 1970)

Vittorio Montano, *L'alta moda italiana, sue realizzazioni e prospettive*, Congresso Nazionale Abbigliamento Autarchia, 1940 Enrica Morini, *Storia della moda XVIII–XX secolo* (Milan, 2000, second edition 2010)

Enrica Morini and Margherita Rosina, *Le donne, la moda, la guerra. Emancipazione femminile e moda durante la Prima guerra mondiale* (Rovereto, 2003)

Diego Mormorio, *Vestiti. Lo stile degli italiani in un secolo di fotografie* (Rome and Bari, 1999)

Benito Mussolini, '*Discorso del 23 marzo XIV in Campidoglio*', in Various Authors, *Per l'indipendenza economica italiana* (Milan, 1937)

Maria Giuseppina Muzzarelli, *Breve storia della moda in Italia* (Bologna, 2011)

Natura, March 1936

Elda Norchi (Futurluce), '*Il voto alla donna*', *Roma Futurista*, no. 13, vol. II, 30 March 1919, in Mondello, 1987, pp.21–2

Umberto Notari, *A che gioco giochiamo? Autarchia contro xenolatria* (Milan, 1938)

Roberta Orsi Landini, '*Gallenga Monaci Maria*', in Vergani, 1999a

Roberta Orsi Landini, '*Alle origini della grande moda italiana. Maria Monaci Gallenga*', in Chiarelli, 2000, pp.30-41

Roberta Orsi Landini (ed.), *Seta. Potere e glamour* (Milan, 2006)

Roberta Orsi Landini and Bruna Niccoli, *Moda a Firenze 1540–1580. Lo stile di Eleonora da Toledo e la sua influenza* (Florence, 2005)

Alfredo Panzini, *La penultima moda, 1850–1930* (Rome, 1930)

Gabriele Parolari, *Abbigliamento* (Milan, 1943)

'Pellicce d'estate', *La Donna*, June 1938

'Pellicce di topo colorato', *Per Voi Signora*, July 1939

Gennaro E. Pistolese, '*Le nuove fibre tessili nazionali*', in Various authors, *L'indipendenza economica italiana* (Milan, 1937), pp.278–92

Mario Praz, selected essays edited by Andrea Cane, *Bellezza e bizzarria* (Milan, 2002)

Prima mostra nazionale della moda, 1933, single issue, *Ente nazionale della moda* (Turin, 1933)

Enrico Quinto and Paolo Tinarelli (eds), *Un secolo di moda. Creazioni e miti del XX secolo* (Milan, 2003)

Relazione del presidente sull'attività svolta durante l'anno 1940, Ente nazionale della moda (Turin, 1941)

Patrizia Ribuoli, 'Le uniformi civili nel regime fascista', in Butazzi, 1980

Stefania Ricci, 'La signorina moderna. Moda ed emancipazione femminile negli Anni Venti', in Various Authors, *Anni Venti. La nascita dell'abito moderno* (Florence, 1991)

Stefania Ricci (ed.), *Museo Salvatore Ferragamo. Materiali per la fantasia* (Florence, 1997)

Stefania Ricci (ed.), *Museo Salvatore Ferragamo. Scarpe e piedi famosi* (Milan, 2000)

Stefania Ricci, *Museo Salvatore Ferragamo. Creatività a colori* (Livorno, 2006)

Lucio Ridenti, *La cavalcata delle stagioni* (Milan, 1962)

'Risorse della moda secondo le discipline dell'abbigliamento', *Bellezza*, November 1941, pp.3–5

Daniel Roche, *La culture des apparences* (Paris, 1989)

Giandomenico Romanelli, 'Mariano Fortuny (tra Ruskin e Proust)', in Maurizio Barberis, Claudio Franzini, Silvio Fuso, and Marco Tosa, *Mariano Fortuny* (Venice, 1999)

Mario Saibante, *Il fascismo e l'industria* (Milan, 1940)

'Salvatore Ferragamo e la moda delle calzature femminili', *L'Illustrazione Italiana*, 17 December 1939

Michelle Sapori, *Rose Bertin. Ministre des modes de Marie-Antoinette* (Paris, 2003)

Francesco Savio, *Ma l'amore no* (Milan, 1975)

Elsa Schiaparelli, *Shocking Life* (London, 1954)

Simona Segre Reinach, *La moda. Un'introduzione* (Rome and Bari, 2005)

Anne-Marie Sohn, 'Between the Wars in France and England', in Duby and Perrot (eds), 1994

Valerie Steele, *Women of Fashion. Twentieth-Century Designers* (New York, 1991)

Valerie Steele (ed.), *Encyclopedia of Clothing and Fashion* (New York, 2005)

'Successi della boutique italiana', *Bellezza*, no. 3, vol. XVIII, March 1957

Umberto Tirelli and Guido Vergani, *Vestire i sogni* (Milan, 1981)

Marco Tosa, *Vestiti da sera 1900–1940* (Modena, 1987)

Roberto Tremelloni, *L'industria tessile italiana come è sorta e come è oggi* (Turin, 1937)

Giovanna Uzzani, 'Per il sole e contro il sole', in Chiarelli, 2003, p.12

Alessandra Vaccari, *La moda nei discorsi dei designer* (Bologna, 2012)

Valentino, in Minnie Gastel, *50 anni di Moda italiana. Breve storia del pret-à-porter* (Milan, 1995)

Bernardo Valli, Benedetta Barzini, and Patrizia Calefato (eds), *Discipline della moda. L'etica dell'apparenza* (Naples, 2003)

Various authors, *I Mostra Nazionale della Moda*, Ente autonomo per la mostra permanente nazionale della moda (Turin, 1933)

Various authors, *II Mostra Nazionale della Moda*, Ente autonomo per la mostra permanente nazionale della moda (Turin, 1933)

Various authors, *La valorizzazione delle fibre tessili nazionali e la moda*, Ente nazionale della moda (Turin, 1936)

Various authors, *Per l'indipendenza economica italiana* (Milan, 1937)

Various authors, *Sperimentazione e moda* (Turin, 1938)

Various authors, *Relazione del Presidente sull'attività svolta nel 1940* (Turin, 1941)

Various authors, *Moda Documento*, Ente nazionale della moda (Turin, 1942)

Various authors, *Torino e l'abbigliamento*, Ente Italiano Moda (Turin, 1966)

Various authors, *Brunetta. Moda, critica, storia* (Parma, 1981)

Various authors, *Anni Trenta. Arte e cultura in Italia* (Milan, 1982)

Various authors, *Annali dell'economia italiana 1930–1938* (Milan, 1983)

Various authors, *Galleria del Costume I* (Florence, 1983)

Various authors, *Roma Capitale 1870–1911. I piaceri e i giorni: la moda* (Venice, 1983)

Various authors, *Il pappagallo giallo* (Florence, 1986)

Various authors, *La Moda Italiana. 1 Le origini dell'Alta Moda e la Maglieria* (Milan, 1987)

Various authors, *Cerimonia a Palazzo. Abiti di corte tra Ottocento e Novecento*, La Galleria del Costume informa 3 (Florence, 1990)

Various authors, *1900–1960. L'alta moda capitale: Torino e le sartorie torinesi* (Milan, 1991)

Various authors, *Per una Storia della Moda pronta* (Florence, 1991)

Various authors, *L'economia italiana tra le due guerre* (Rome, 1994)

Various authors, *Abiti in festa l'ornamento e la sartoria italiana* (Livorno, 1996)

Various authors, *Thayaht. Un artista alle origini del made in Italy* (Prato, 2007)

Various authors, *Salvatore Ferragamo. Evolving Legend 1928–2008* (Milan, 2008)

Various authors, *Moda in Italia. 150 anni di eleganza 1861–2011* (Milan, 2011)

Vera, 'La moda: commenti e consigli', *Lidel*, June 1932

Vera, 'La moda alla Mostra di Torino', *Lidel*, May 1933

Vera, 'La moda italiana vista a Firenze', *Novità*, no. 83, September 1957

Guido Vergani (ed), *Maria Pezzi. Una vita dentro la moda* (Milano, 1998)

Guido Vergani, *Dizionario della moda* (Milan, 1999a, second edition 2003; third edition 2009)

Guido Vergani, 'Biki, la signora della moda', *Il Corriere della Sera*, 25 February 1999b

Angela Völker, *Moda Wiener Werkstätte* (Florence, 1990)

Giuseppe Volpi Di Misurata, *Industria e autarchia,* Fascist Confederation of Industrialists (Rome, 1937)

Volt, 'Manifesto della moda femminile futurista', *Roma Futurista*, 29 February 1920

Linda Welters and Abby Lillethun (eds), *The Fashion Reader* (Oxford and New York, 2011)

Diana Vreeland, *D.V.* (New York, 1984)

Nicola White, *Reconstructing Italian Fashion: America and the Development of the Italian Fashion Industry* (Oxford and New York, 2000)

Elizabeth Wilson, *Adorned in Dreams: Fashion and Modernity* (London, 2003)

Sabrina Zannier, *1968/70 come terminus ad quem della società del benessere e dell'ottimismo e come terminus a quo di una nuova povertà*, in Silvia Grandi, Alessandra Vaccari and Sabrina Zannier, *La moda nel secondo dopoguerra* (Bologna, 1992)

Index

Index   111

Acknowledgements

For the images and other vital information, I would like to thank Osvaldo Avallone, Barbara Bertozzi, Elisabetta Caprotti, Marella Caracciolo Chia, Rossella Caracciolo Sleiter, Simona Chiappa, Caterina Chiarelli, Letizia De Angelis, Daniela Degl'Innocenti, Antonella Di Marco, Maria Cristina Di Martino, Paola Garavaglia, Maria Luce Gargallo, Patrizia Gatti, Cristina Ghergo, Bonizza Giordani Aragno, Pangasio Gnoli, Umberto Gnoli, Tullio Gregory, Maria Luisa Jacini, Lupo Lanzara, Michela Laurora, Silvia Luperini, Francesca Marani, Andrea Mattone, Flaminia Nardone, Carla Oliva Fonteni, Teresa Parruccini, Maria Luisa Patrizi Montoro, Innocenzo and Umberta Patrizi Montoro, Paola Pisa, Stefania Ricci, Filippo and Moira Nicolis di Robilant, Roberto Roncalli, Rossana Rummo, Adriana Sartogo, Betta Seeber Calamai, Francesco Solinas, Giorgia Sparavigna, Giuseppe Sperandio, Margherita Taticchi, Maddalena Torricelli, Mauro Tosti Croce, Elena Valentino and Verde Visconti.

Thanks also to the Academy of Costume and Fashion, the Alessandrina Library, the Fondazione Biagiotti Cigna, the Costume Gallery at the Palazzo Pitti, Fendi, the Ghergo Archive, the Giordani Aragno Archive, Gucci, the National Library of Rome, the Nicolis di Robilant Archive, Prada, the Salvatore Ferragamo Museum, the Taticchi Archive and the Textile Museum in Prato.

I would also like to thank Philip Contos, Elizabeth Currie, Mark Eastment, Reena Kataria, Susan North, Lucia Savi and Alexandra Stetter for their invaluable help. I am very grateful to Gianluca Mori and Gian Carlo Brioschi at Carocci Editore, who have supported me in this project.

Above all, I would like to thank Sonnet Stanfill. The concept of this book – to provide an overview to accompany the exhibition *The Glamour of Italian Fashion 1945–2014* at the Victoria and Albert Museum – was developed with her encouragement.

Picture credits